LUFTWAFFE FIGHTER PILOT

LUFTWAFFE FIGHTER PILOT

Defending the Reich against the RAF
and the USAAF

WOLFGANG FISCHER
Edited and Translated by John Weal

Grub Street • London

Published by
Grub Street
4 Rainham Close
London
SW11 6SS

British Library Cataloguing in Publication Data
  Fischer, Wolfgang.
  Luftwaffe fighter pilot : defending the Reich against the
  RAF and USAAF.
  1. Fischer, Wolfgang. 2. Germany. Luftwaffe--History.
  3. World War, 1939-1945--Personal narratives, German.
  4. World War, 1939-1945--Aerial operations, German.
  5. Fighter pilots--Germany--Biography.
  I. Title
  940.5'44943'092-dc22

ISBN-13: 9781906502836

Cover design and typesetting by Sarah Driver
Edited by Sophie Campbell
Printed and bound by MPG Ltd, Bodmin, Cornwall

Grub Street Publishing only uses
FSC (Forest Stewardship Council) paper for its books.

CONTENTS

PREFACE

'Yellow 1' lurched violently as the flak shell burst close alongside. Pieces of shrapnel tore into the fuselage and engine cowling. I knew instinctively that this was it, and half expected to see my past life flash before my eyes. But training took over. Hauling the stick back into my stomach, I pointed the nose of the Focke-Wulf skywards. I desperately needed to gain altitude, not only to escape the tracer being hosed up at me from the armada of ships beneath my wings, but also to give myself sufficient height to bale out.

As I climbed, still under fire, I unbuckled my seat harness and disconnected the radio leads. Judging the time to be right, and before the labouring engine gave up the ghost altogether, I jettisoned the canopy and kicked the stick forwards. The machine bucked and I was catapulted clean out of the cockpit. Buffeted by the slipstream, I was thrown against the tailplane, but scarcely noticed what I took to be a glancing blow on my left shoulder.

We had flown a wide arc out to sea before mounting our attack and now, fortunately, a stiff offshore breeze was carrying me towards the coastline. But I still couldn't be sure whether I was going to come down in the shallows or make it to dry land. As I drifted closer, and despite the light flak that continued to flick past dangerously close to my parachute, I found myself reflecting on the twenty-three-year journey – the last five of those years in Luftwaffe uniform – that had brought me to my present predicament descending helplessly towards the Normandy invasion beaches...

Chapter 1

A CAREFREE CHILDHOOD

Fate, in the guise of my father's career, decreed that I should be born in Waldthurn, a tiny community in the heart of the Upper Palatinate Forest some seventy-five kilometres north of Regensburg. The date was 30 October 1921. Less than three years had passed since the end of the Great War, and the aftermath of that conflict had brought sweeping changes to this sleepy backwater region of northeastern Bavaria. Its near neighbours, citizens of the collapsed Austro-Hungarian Empire, spoke the same language; even the same local dialect. For centuries the two sides, Bavarian and Bohemian, had co-existed as part of the Holy Roman Empire. Now Bohemia found itself incorporated into the newly established state of Czechoslovakia – brought into being by the post-war treaties of Versailles, St. Germain and Trianon – and enclosed behind a rigidly enforced frontier. It was my father's duties as a customs official on the Czech border that had brought the family to Waldthurn.

But Bavaria had undergone changes too. Following the Great War it lost its status as an independent kingdom. As part of the new German republic it had to forfeit a number of sovereign rights, including control of its own borders, the responsibility for which now passed into the hands of central government. Although a patriotic German, father allowed his Bavarian heart to rule his head and declined the offer to remain in the service of the state. Our brief sojourn in Waldthurn thus came to an abrupt end. Apparently father received an indemnity which, although not exactly generous, enabled him to brave the very bleak economic situation prevailing in Germany at this time and take the plunge into the commercial world. Having studied political economy and business administration in the course of his civil service career, he landed a job as manager of a sawmill in Miesbach, a small town to the southeast of Munich.

Not yet three years old, I have no recollection at all of the family's move in 1924. But not long afterwards – I must by then have been in my second year at the local primary school – I got my first childish insight into the political turbulence that was already beginning to jeopardize Germany's fragile young democracy. It transpired that one of father's colleagues at the sawmill, the man in charge of the company's books, was apparently siphoning off some of the profits for himself. As soon as father got wind of this he fired the man on the spot. The miscreant turned up at our house the following day accompanied by his brother and, after some heated words had been exchanged, declared himself a communist. Accusing father of being a 'capitalist lackey', he demanded his job back, claiming he had the full support of the KPD, or German Communist Party.

This didn't go down at all well with my father and the proceedings quickly developed into a free-for-all. Unfortunately for the avowed communist, his brother was rather small and slight of stature and this lent something of a comic air to the ensuing brawl. With his left hand father grabbed the weedy sibling by the back of his braces and lifted him clear off his feet. Held face down just above the floor, arms and legs flailing, he could do little more than squeal loudly while father brought matters to a swift conclusion by delivering a series of well-aimed right-handers to his remaining opponent.

Nor should mother's part in this fracas go unrecorded. Becoming aware of the increasing commotion, and fearing no good would come of it, she had rushed into the bedroom to get the Browning pistol that father had 'liberated' from a Tommy officer on the western front. Reappearing moments later, she planted herself heroically behind the struggling trio and began fumbling with the unfamiliar 'indoors cannon'. By then, thank God, father had the situation well in hand and she was not called upon to use it. Had she done so, she would very likely have drilled holes through all three of them. Having witnessed the entire episode, I later asked father what a communist was. He told me that they were 'enemies of the state'. Since then I have always had something against communists.

It was not until our next move, which took us to Thansau on the east bank of the River Inn some ten kilometres south of Rosenheim, that the world began to open up for me. The year was 1928, I was nearing the end of my time in primary school, and it was the dawn of what people were optimistically calling the 'New Age'. But I was not yet old enough to have any idea of what this new age held in store for us. I spent my childhood in what can only be described as one large playground.

Some of my happiest memories revolve around the Inn itself. In those days the river had not yet been harnessed by the series of weirs that have since been constructed to the south of Rosenheim – right by Thansau, in fact. In my time it tumbled freely down from the narrow valleys of the Alps, flowing through Rosenheim and northwards to join the Danube at Passau. There was just one small dam, sufficient to tame it during the high water period when the snows melted in the High Alps. This prevented it from flooding the stretch of broad wooded valley where our house and land was situated. In the summer months its waters, clear, shallow and fast flowing, ran between exposed banks of shingle. But in the late spring, at the height of the snowmelt, it became an angry rushing torrent, the colour of sand. The noise of its passage could be heard from afar. Hemmed in by thick woods on either side, it presented an almost primeval picture far removed from our twentieth century civilization.

When the late spring surge subsided, however, it left behind numerous small pools, which in high summer became as warm as bath water. My friends and I paddled and played about in these for hours. Our imaginations fired by father's tales of his days in colonial Africa before the war, and of the crocodiles that lurked along the muddy banks of the rivers there, we would splash and thrash about in the pure, silvery fine-grained sand of the Inn fighting 'river monsters' of every kind. Every time we returned home after these battles mother would have to put us straight into the bath to wash away the river sand that still covered us from head to foot.

The woods stretched a good 300 metres eastwards from the nearby dam. A fair sized stream ran through the trees and this marked the boundary of our property, which encompassed an area of about 24,000 square metres. When we moved in, much of this was also thickly wooded. And as it was neither cultivated nor forested, it formed what today might be termed one enormous biotope, consisting mainly of alders standing among a near impenetrable carpet of bushes, shrubs and reeds. Raspberries and blackberries also grew in abundance and we became enthusiastic fruit pickers, taking most of our booty home for mother to make into jam. This otherwise undisturbed paradise was home to a myriad of creatures, including hares, squirrels, pine martens, partridges and pheasants. To us children it was a place of enchantment.

A CAREFREE CHILDHOOD

There was, however, one drawback to our house being so close to the river: the height of the water table was governed entirely by its state. When the Inn was in spate our cellars could be anything up to one metre deep in water. But we children didn't look upon this as any kind of disadvantage. Quite the opposite, in fact, for it gave us the chance to 'sail' from one cellar room to the other in mother's large washtub.

When we moved to Thansau father was forty-seven years old and he soon began to devote all his spare time to clearing and cultivating the woodland on our property. Completely unaided he created a large meadow, which he then leased to the Schlossmann family who owned the neighbouring estate. He also laid out an extensive strawberry field and cleared a thirty-metre wide strip of grass along the southern frontage of the house for us to play on. On this plot he then dug – entirely by hand – two swimming pools, each measuring fifteen metres by five metres, and each three metres deep. The existing ground water quickly filled both pools to a depth of one-and-a-half metres and, as this underground water flowed northwards along the line of the Inn at a rate of about one metre a day, the pools did not become brackish but remained naturally free of bacteria and any chemical impurities. The topsoil only went down some thirty centimetres before giving way to the finest Inn sand. This kept the bottom of the pools spotlessly clean, but was immediately swirled up in billowing clouds whenever we splashed about – so after every session in the pool it was back to mother and straight into the bath again for another scrub down!

The felling of the trees was always a special event, although now that I was getting on in years it meant that I had to pull my weight on one end of the large, two-man saw. But the climax every time was the blowing up of the stump. As a front-line soldier of the Great War, father knew a thing or two about high explosives. After he had carefully packed the blast holes with black powder, the shutters on the windows of the house would be closed while we children had to run around the neighbourhood warning people of the impending explosion – sadly, father flatly refused to buy a signal trumpet to relieve us of this task. Then there would be an almighty bang, clouds of smoke and copious amounts of sand would fly into the air and the offending stump, together with its roots, could be effortlessly hauled out of the ground. When tackling the first stumps, those nearest the house, large clods of dirt and muck would sometimes get stuck to the walls and these we would then have laboriously to scrape and wash off.

The sound of father's activities could, of course, be heard throughout Thansau. If the wind was right, the noise might even reach as far as Rohrdorf, three kilometres away. But people would simply remark 'Aha, the Hauptmann's up to his old tricks again!' – father was always referred to as the 'Hauptmann', this being the rank he held when he returned home from the war – and that was all the notice that would be taken. One can't help wondering what the reaction would be today if people went around letting off high explosives in the course of their everyday lives. But then we lived in a different age, although we didn't perhaps realize at the time just how idyllic everything was.

But it wasn't all paradise. There was also school to be attended. Our school was in Rohrdorf and boasted all of two rooms; one for classes one-three, and the other for four-eight. The head teacher, Herr Birkner – who was rumoured to be a 'Sozi' or Socialist – ruled with a rod of iron. The slightest misdemeanour could result in being caned on the open palm of the hand or being made to kneel in the corner of the classroom for fifteen minutes on a sharp-edged piece of firewood. The wood was there ostensibly to feed the stove, but Herr Birkner had his own peculiar ideas on educational therapy.

In both summer and winter we made the journey to and from

school on foot. The trip home could sometimes take as long as two-and-a-half hours, for we often played a favourite game on the way. For a good part of the distance the winding country road – in those days not yet metalled and still little more than a dirt track – ran alongside the single-track railway line to Frasdorf. Having armed ourselves with a plentiful supply of caps for our toy pistols, we would lay these out along the rail over a length of several metres and eagerly await the approach of the train. When the tiny locomotive, known locally as the 'Frasdorf Billygoat', ran over the carefully spaced pellets it would sound to all the world like a long burst of machine-gun fire. The crew of the 'Billygoat' joined in the fun, the driver and fireman laughing and waving as they rat-tat-tatted past us. But they were not quite so amused when we had no caps and put stones on the rail instead. This practice came to a sudden end when our parents somehow got to hear of it and delivered a few well-deserved clips around our collective ears.

In 1931 I passed the entrance examination for the Rosenheim Classical Grammar School and, although we would continue to live at Thansau for five more years, things were no longer quite so carefree. My new school was a good eight kilometres from home and walking was no longer an option, so my parents bought me a brand new bicycle. It was an 'Express' model bearing that company's distinctive leaping greyhound trademark, as I can still clearly recall. This I used during the summer months. In the winter I was allowed to travel back and forth on the 'Frasdorf Billygoat'. But the journeys I enjoyed most of all were on those days when father had business in Rosenheim and rode into town on his second-hand 200cc DKW motorbike, known to the family as 'Schnauferl', or 'Wheezer'. Always a practical man, father would bring a towrope with him on these occasions. He would collect me from school, tie the rope securely to the front of my 'Express', and tow me home. To the best of my recollection we never had a single mishap.

It was my father who had selected my new school, as he himself had enjoyed a similar classical education when he was a boy.
But the fees of thirty Reichsmarks were quite a lot for those days
and represented very nearly ten per cent of my parents' income.
And when my sister Radegunde – 'Rada' to the family – who
was two years younger than me, entered the Rosenheim High
School for Girls in 1933, another thirty Reichsmarks had to be
found for her. But 1933 was also the year that Adolf Hitler came
to power and the new regime implemented many of its promised social reforms remarkably quickly. Among the first meas-
ures to be introduced was the halving of school fees for a
family's second child and their abolition altogether for all subsequent children.

Another sign of Hitler's taking office was a sudden huge expansion in the country's road building programme. This
prompted father seriously to consider the idea of getting the
family more comfortably motorized by replacing the motorbike
with a car. Brochures were obtained and pored over, this make
was compared to that, dealers were visited, and some even came
out to Thansau to try to persuade father to choose their particular model. In the end, the favourite turned out to be the DKW
Reichsklasse costing 1,800 Marks. This just pipped the Opel
Olympia, which had been the front-runner up until then.

But Herr Vodermayer, who ran the Opel dealership in Rosenheim, was clearly not a man to give up easily. He arrived at the
house to plead his case, but must have got under father's skin
in a big way. The discussion grew more and more heated and
ended with my father chasing the terrified dealer out of the
house and along the front path calling him all the names under
the sun. 'Arsehole', he growled furiously as he stomped back indoors. And so our modest but faithful 'Schnauferl' continued to
serve all our transport needs. Father even allowed me and my

school friends to use it – more accurately perhaps, misuse it – to roar around between the fruit trees in the orchard he had planted.

But one of our expeditions, now part of family history, was to prove too much even for the sadly no longer so trusty steed. It was 1933, the summer holidays were looming, and plans were made for a trip to the Saarland to visit Aunt Margarethe and her husband, Uncle Fritz, who had been a fighter pilot in the Great War. Father decided that the journey should be turned into an adventure and that, while mother and Rada were packed off to the Saarland by train, he and I would make our way there on his motorbike. And so early one morning, with me planted firmly on the pillion seat, we cheerfully set off. I must admit to having felt a bit nervous, not without good reason as it transpired, but the weather was fine and promised to remain so.

Our route was to take us from Thansau, via Füssen, to Lake Constance. From there we would follow the Rhine Valley northwards before branching west through the Pfalz to our holiday destination in the Saarland; it was a journey of over 700 kilometres. Father had calculated that it would take us three days to complete the outward journey, and he was allowing two for the return trip. The first minor hiccup occurred outside Füssen where the engine, due perhaps to the combination of a not altogether adequate service and the warmth of the summer sun, overheated and simply died on us. Father didn't take this too seriously. He wrapped the cylinder in fresh grass, which I then had to replace at regular intervals. This allowed it to cool off while we sat in the welcome shade of a large tree and tucked into our sandwiches.

The 'repair' actually worked and we were soon able to continue on our way towards Lake Constance where, if memory serves me right, we stopped for the night. By about noon the next day, with the sun beating down even more fiercely, we had

The author's father poses proudly next to 'Schnauferl' ready to
set off on the expedition to the Saarland. The author is on the
balcony behind (second left).

reached the district of Swabia and father was keeping an eye out
for a source of drinking water as our supplies were running dangerously low. In one village he parked the machine and me beneath a linden tree and went from house to house to ask for
water. But not a door opened. People simply watched us
through closed windows. Nobody was prepared to give us a single drop. I could see the sweat pouring down father's forehead.
His face was getting redder and redder, the veins were starting
to stand out and I knew exactly what was coming – he was
about to fly into one of his legendary rages.

Striding back into the middle of the village square, father
drew himself up to his full height and began, at the top of his
voice, to hurl insults at the entire community. A barrage of in-

vective in his broadest Bavarian left the locals in little doubt as to what he thought of them. He was soon in full swing, "... and you can't even spare us a single glass of water, you lousy Swabian skinflints, hiding there in those manure heaps you call home along with your chickens and pigs. Well, you can keep your filthy pisswater – and while you're at it, you can kiss my arse sideways!!"

It was at this juncture that several doors opened and four burly figures armed with pitchforks began to advance towards us. "Papa," I said anxiously, "I really think we ought to leave." Faced with this new development, father had little option but to agree. He kick-started 'Schnauferl'. Fortunately the bike's engine sprang into life immediately and we were able to make our getaway. At the next village we came to we stopped at an inn where we were given a very friendly reception. Our image of Swabia was restored in an instant. Not all its inhabitants were as dour and unwelcoming as those we had first had the misfortune to encounter.

In the evening we arrived at Annweiler, a small town in the Pfalz nestling beneath the Trifels, the ruined fortress where England's King Richard the Lionheart had been held captive in the twelfth century. Father had a weakness for historical locations and it was here that we stayed overnight. The next morning did not begin very well. Neither of us was unduly surprised when the DKW flatly refused to fire. After trying to kick-start it into life a good fifty times, father – never one to throw money around unnecessarily – next decided that we should attempt to hill-start our recalcitrant steed instead. We must have rolled down one of Annweiler's steepest streets at least another twenty times, and pushed the machine back up to the top again puffing and sweating as it grew progressively heavier, before father finally admitted defeat.

Luckily there was a garage-cum-workshop nearby. And inside it stood something on four wheels that, even in those far-off days, could only be described as an old crock. I noticed that father was eyeing this heap of junk covetously, no doubt fearing – with some justification – that our troubles with 'Schnauferl' were far from over. The dealer was also quick to spot father's interest, stating that he could be persuaded to part with the thing for the princely sum of 300 Reichsmarks. I dared to protest strongly at this, declaring that no amount of money in the world would tempt me to climb aboard the prehistoric contraption. My unexpected outburst resulted in father's deciding to drop the whole deal and instead invest two Reichsmarks in a new spark plug. Thus rejuvenated, our two-wheeled sledge conveyed us the remaining 150 kilometres to our destination, Mittelbexbach, without the slightest hitch.

When the holidays were over we all set off home at the same time, mother and sister again by train so that they could be back in Thansau to prepare for our arrival two days later. Our first day on the road passed uneventfully – until the final kilometre before our planned overnight stop. This was somewhere along Swabia's Jagst Valley; I can no longer remember the name of the place but, knowing father, I'm sure it had a historical connotation. The road was one long gradient down to the floor of the valley, where it made a sharp left-hand turn into the village street. We arrived at the top of the hill. It was a pleasant summer's evening and we could almost taste the delicious home-cooked meal that would be waiting for us at the inn below.

As usual, father was wearing his traditional Bavarian headgear with its tuft of chamois hair back-to-front in order to prevent its being blown off his head. And below his lederhosen he kept his bare knees pointed slightly outwards to avoid getting burned by the engine's single cylinder. It was his custom at the top of every incline to switch off the ignition and coast downhill to save petrol. This time was no exception and we had already picked up quite a speed when we saw ahead of us, just before the left-hand bend, two fully laden oxcarts emerging on to the road from fields on either side. The two women leading the ox teams were making for the middle of the road, clearly intending to have a good chat as they walked their charges back to the village. They remained completely oblivious to father's frantic hooting as we bore down upon them. In their defence, it must be said that he was pressing the bulb of the horn so violently that it had broken and was emitting little more than the occasional pitiful squeak.

"Papa," I yelled in panic, "now we're for it!" "Just hold on tight to me, son," he shouted. I hunched down behind his broad back in the forlorn hope that, when the inevitable collision occurred, I could cling on to him as we sailed through the air and perhaps land fairly softly. An absurd idea, I now freely admit, but one that I'm sure helped me survive the next few seconds. But we actually made it! There couldn't have been much more than a metre separating the two women as we flashed past between them. The moment we had done so I looked back over my shoulder and caught a glimpse of the two pairs of oxen galloping back into the fields – one to the left, the other to the right – with the two screaming women chasing after them. Now on the flat, father laid the DKW elegantly into the left-hand curve and braked to a stop in front of the inn. I was shaking like a leaf, but father still seemed remarkably calm. In an uncharacteristically tender gesture, he ruffled my hair. As a father myself now, I can appreciate how he must really have been feeling.

Things were much quieter the following day. The weather was near perfect and the DKW purred contentedly along the country roads – the autobahns had not yet been built – as we headed towards Munich. There we suffered yet another spark-plug problem. Although there was a garage close by, father of course insisted on trying to sort it out himself. We had stopped for a brief rest by the peace monument up on the right bank of the River Isar, and he decided that the long straight slope back down to the Luitpold Bridge would be ideal for getting 'Schnauferl' going again. However, after the fifth attempt had failed to achieve the desired effect – "I told you so, Papa" – father had to admit defeat and we wheeled the DKW to the garage we had seen earlier.

Some expert assistance, plus a replacement plug, soon had our motorbike back in full working order. Before we continued on our way, father declared that he needed a quick mouthful of brandy from the bottle granny had given him when we left Mittelbexbach and which, he was sure, had been stowed in the toolbox between the two saddles. Unfortunately he was wrong in his assumption and instead took a hefty swig from the brandy bottle in which he kept his emergency supply of engine oil. His reaction can be imagined. But with the home stretch now beckoning, his good humour was soon restored.

After a good two hours we had passed through Rosenheim and were humming along the road leading to the turn-off for Thansau and home. We bumped across the railway tracks and headed for the little bridge across the stream that bordered our property. Mother and Rada were standing on the balcony waving excitedly and we waved back with equal gusto. Maybe father overdid it, or perhaps he should have paid more attention to the bridge. We started to wobble, father couldn't regain control of the machine, and we went into the water with an almighty splash. Father and I scrambled clear of the motorbike, which sank, hissing, spitting and gurgling beneath the surface. Father's hat started to float off downstream, but I quickly retrieved it. He gave it a couple of shakes and defiantly placed it back on his head. But the effect was no longer the same. The once-proud tuft of chamois hair now looked more like a bedraggled paintbrush.

I had been dimly aware of the horrified shrieks coming from the balcony as we went into the water. Mother and Rada rushed across to us, followed by several neighbours who had also heard the commotion. Luckily, the stream below the bridge was not very deep and the DKW was soon dragged on to dry land with the aid of some ropes. Father tipped it from side to side to get rid of most of the water, but it had to go into the local garage for seven days to be fully repaired – a well-earned week's rest for 'Schnauferl' after its recent gallant performance.

CHAPTER 2

GROWING UP IN THE 'NEW AGE'

Unlike my father's generation, I had been too young to understand the turmoil and unrest that had plagued the Weimar Republic. And so, although I became increasingly aware of the political changes that occurred after Hitler's assumption of power in 1933, I was in no position to form a balanced judgement on them, as I had nothing to compare them against. My peers and I – the generation coming of age under the new dictatorship – saw no reason to question the status quo. Our families, indeed the whole country, seemed to be prospering. Living standards were improving. We couldn't imagine anything different; but then we weren't being offered any alternatives.

In fact, my father had established a small group of like-minded nationalist supporters at Waldthurn as far back as 1922. Their aims closely paralleled the views later propounded by Hitler. They wanted a revision of what they considered to be the iniquitous terms of the Versailles Treaty, and the formation of a nationalist social state strong enough to counter the rising tide of Bolshevism, whose threats of a 'world revolution' were the stuff of nightmares for the bourgeois classes of central and western Europe.

But father's beliefs were not unconditional and his outspokenness proved not just detrimental to his advancement; on occasion it would pose a very real danger to his continued well-being. His attitude towards national-socialism was so positive at the outset that he had no qualms about joining the party. But after 1933, with the regime becoming ever more totalitarian, he in turn became – if not entirely 'anti' – certainly increasingly disaffected. He disliked the loud-mouthed posturing of many minor officials, or 'party jackasses' as he called them, and was appalled at the discrimination being shown against the Jews, which he feared would have severe political repercussions abroad. But what stretched his loyalty to the limit was the infamous 'Röhm-putsch' of June 1933 when Ernst Röhm and many leading members of the SA were summarily executed.

Father made his feelings about the murder of Röhm and his colleagues all too clear to a number of high-ranking party officials of his acquaintance. Not wishing to lose his support, these latter felt compelled to send somebody to visit us at Thansau to smooth father's ruffled feathers. They could not have chosen a worse emissary. It was the local district leader, or Ortsgruppenleiter, a pompous braggart whom father couldn't stand at any price. He was one of the so-called 'March violets', the nickname given to those opportunists who had quickly jumped aboard the party bandwagon in the weeks immediately after Hitler's appointment as Reich chancellor in January 1933. And this was the individual being sent to make father 'see reason'! It was a recipe for disaster – and that is exactly what it turned out to be.

The guest was ushered into the large drawing room while mother, Rada and I sat in the kitchen across the hall awaiting the inevitable explosion. The conversation got louder by the minute until only father could be heard yelling at the top of his voice. Then the door of the drawing room flew open and father bundled the portly district leader out of the house and down the front steps. In the ruckus the 'party jackass' lost his leather belt and gold-braided cap, and these father tossed contemptuously after him. He made off uttering dire threats of retribution, but his complaints must have fallen upon deaf ears in higher circles for, as far as I am aware, no further action was ever taken.

The party could perhaps tolerate the odd maverick in its ranks during those early days as it was already looking ahead to the future and had its sights set firmly on the young. By 'volunteering' to join one of the two youth movements for boys – the 'Jungvolk' for those up to the age of fourteen, and the 'Hitlerjugend' for those aged between fourteen and eighteen – almost the entire rising generation of German youth came under the national and ideological influences of the new regime. It was possible to escape the worst of these influences, however, by opting for one of the three technical subdivisions of the Hitler Youth: the motorized, flying or naval sections.

When I turned fifteen I joined the 'Flieger-Hitlerjugend' or 'Flieger-HJ' – not, I must confess, driven by any sense of revolt, but simply because I was fascinated by the idea of flying. And I can honestly say that I cannot recall receiving any overt party political training as such; perhaps the powers-that-be were too clever for that. We were following Hitler's lead willingly enough anyway. It was just the everyday propaganda that passed us by.

During the summer months membership of the Flieger-HJ entailed turning up at the group's 'hangar' once a week. Here we began by building model aircraft and flying them in competition. Later we were allowed to help with the maintenance and repair of the glider flown by the older boys. In the winter, after the fields had been harvested and when the weather permitted, there would be flying practice at least twice a month.

Our flight instructor was 'Papa' Seitz. He had been a pilot during the Great War and was really like a father figure to us.

Financial resources in the Flieger-HJ were not exactly abundant to begin with, and grew progressively less the further down the organizational table you went. In a small district group like ours this was reflected in the equipment we had. Take, for example, the antiquated old truck that was pressed into service to transport us out to the practice slopes in the Bavarian hills or the lower Alpine regions of the Tyrol. This appeared to have started its working life as a brewer's dray. To the rear of the wooden, box-like driver's cab was an open flatbed body, some four metres in length, upon which we used to huddle together shivering with cold despite our warm winter clothing. Behind us on a rickety trailer was our pride and joy: a Grunau G9 glider; the notorious 'skull-splitter', so called on account of the sturdy wooden brace located only a matter of centimetres in front of the pilot's face.

It was the ambition of every budding glider pilot to gain the coveted C-Class certificate, the highest of the three grades of proficiency – A, B and C – that could be won. But the rather primitive and bulky Grunau G9 would only permit us to attain Grade B. And for me even this achievement still lay many months ahead. My first 'flights', in fact, consisted of nothing more than being dragged across the ground in order to familiarize me with the take-off procedure. Nevertheless, each drag was proudly recorded in my hitherto pristine flying logbook with the appropriate letter 'R', indicating 'Rutsch', or slide.

In addition to our flying activities, which, had we but known it, were regarded by our lords and masters as 'pre-military training', we were also required to join with the general Hitler Youth in field exercises. Armed with watches and compasses, and weighed down by full backpacks, two sides –Blue and Red – would have to find and do battle with each other in open country. Target practice, at first with air rifles and later with small calibre weapons, was also carried out in the nearby butts under strict military supervision.

Another part of the youth welfare programme was the lengthy outings. These were, in essence, conducted youth tours. Costing the participants very little, they took groups of youngsters to various parts of Germany. Ostensibly intended to bring the inhabitants of the different regions into closer contact with each other, this was a not altogether bad idea – had it not been for the inevitable ideological undertones. Such subtleties were lost on us, however. We simply regarded these excursions as thrilling adventures. I well remember one such fourteen-day trip to the North Sea coast. Having travelled to Hamburg by train, we set off to march along the dykes to the Danish border.

For us landlubbers, who had never seen a body of water any larger than a Bavarian lake, the trek northwards along the Schleswig-Holstein coastline was an amazing experience. We marched in all weathers, in rain and storms, and I can still recall the salty tang of the sea air as what, to us, seemed like huge tidal waves smashed themselves against the sloping flanks of the dykes almost at our feet. At a camp near Leck, just short of Denmark, we spent a few days under canvas before catching the train home from Flensburg. Such trips were huge fun for all of us. We were off the streets and were able to do things and see places that our parents could otherwise never have afforded. We were living for the present and enjoying it immensely. That things might get darker in the future didn't even cross our minds.

Meanwhile, I continued with my studies at Rosenheim grammar school, just as generations of pupils have done before and since. For we were still just schoolboys at heart, and not above playing silly pranks on our teachers. One particular bit of tomfoolery was at the expense of our form master, Professor Michel.

It was a warm day and my friend Hansi, who was usually the instigator of such antics, suggested that just before the lesson was about to begin we should all climb out of the windows (our classroom was up on the first floor) and crouch down out of sight on the wide ledge that ran beneath them. The corner window was partially covered by a curtain and one of our number was chosen to keep watch behind this and carefully note Michel's reaction. Punctually at the start of the lesson the door opened. Our victim took three steps into the room and came to a dead stop. He looked at his watch, went back outside to check the number on the door, came back in again, took another look at his watch, shook his head in bafflement and disappeared.

As soon as he had closed the door behind him we quickly clambered back inside and took our places at our desks. A few minutes later Michel returned with the headmaster, Dr. Reich. Our form master strode into the room with an indignant look on his face, and again stopped as if rooted to the spot. "Well, what seems to be the problem, Herr Professor?" the headmaster queried, "They are all here as far as I can see." "But there wasn't a soul present just now," Michel spluttered in total bewilderment. Dr. Reich turned to the class prefect, "What's this all about, Häckl?" "I'm afraid I have no idea, Herr Oberstudiendirektor. Everyone was here waiting for the lesson to begin when Herr Professor Michel walked into the room, glanced at his watch and walked out again." Michel was about to explode, but the headmaster simply said, "Let's leave things for now, Herr Professor. Come and see me after the lesson." Dr. Reich must have guessed what had been going on, and presumably persuaded our form master to let the matter drop.

Minor insubordinations became increasingly frequent as the political situation began to make itself felt even in the enclosed world of our grammar school. The demands made upon our time by Hitler Youth activities were encroaching more and more on our normal school hours. Short-sightedly, we of course much preferred the exciting diversions offered by the Hitler Youth to the boring business of studying. On occasion we would even deliberately provoke such 'clashes of interest', secure in the knowledge that it was nearly always the school authorities that had to give way.

The private political leanings of the teaching staff were also coming under scrutiny. This was brought home to us when one of the form masters, the kindly old 'Poodle' Pedell, was replaced by a young man wearing a party badge, who – I now firmly believe – was put in place to report on the other teachers. One of these, 'Papa' Fink, who taught Latin to the first and second formers, was rumoured to have left-wing tendencies, although he never admitted as much. Another, Professor Ruckdeschel, a somewhat awkward and clumsy individual, was an unashamedly committed follower of Hitler. He would bring the *Völkischer Beobachter*, the official newspaper of the Nazi party, into class with him and read one or two of the day's articles out aloud to us. Our mathematics teacher Professor Hämmerlein, who had fought in the Great War, was more circumspect. He was the only one to pour cold water on our high spirits. "Just wait," he warned us, "when the guns start going off you'll soon start singing a different tune."

But his words fell on deaf ears. There was too much to see and to do. It was not long after this that our small Flieger-HJ group was given the chance to play a part in the 1936 'Deutschlandflug', the annual competitive air rally that toured almost every part of Germany. We jumped at the offer and were taken to nearby Prien airfield, close to Lake Chiem, which was one of the stops on the Bavarian leg of the competition. The small grass field was packed with dozens of light aircraft of every kind. We had never seen so many machines in one place before. Our duties were purely menial, of course. We washed windscreens and cabin windows, cleaned the floors of the cockpits and helped push those aircraft making an overnight stop into the hangar.

But the experience whetted our appetites for the world of flying even more – this no doubt being the whole object of the exercise – and, as an added bonus, we got to see some of the leading sports pilots of the day: people like Hanna Reitsch, Elly Beinhorn and the head of the National Socialist Flying Corps, General Friedrich Christiansen. Before leaving Prien each of us was presented with a large oval plaque inscribed Deutschlandflug 1936 in recognition of our efforts.

1936 was an altogether eventful year for the Fischer family. We moved into our new house in Rosenheim and father went to work in South Africa. The plot of land in Rosenheim was much smaller than the one we were leaving behind at Thansau, although by today's standards it was still large, measuring a good 3,000 square metres. The house itself was amply big enough for the four of us. Surrounded by greenery, it was within easy walking distance of the town centre. It offered far less scope for outdoor activities than we had become accustomed to at Thansau. But this was no longer quite so important. Our childish games of cowboys and Indians had by this time given way to more grown-up pursuits.

Father's trip to Africa came about as a direct result of the political climate we were living in. The Schlossmanns, the Jewish family who owned the farm estate next door to us at Thansau, had become good friends. They had four children, two boys and two girls, of whom the elder of each was about the same age as my sister and myself. Helmut, the oldest boy, was in the class below me at school. His sister Edith attended the secondary modern school in Rosenheim. Sometimes, on warm sunny days, their maternal grandmother, Frau Bondy, would arrange for her chauffeur to pick us all up from school and drive us out to Lake Sims to go swimming. Sitting in the back of Frau Bondy's large limousine, which the uniformed chauffeur was allowed to drive no faster than fifty kilometres per hour, we two Fischer children felt as if we had finally arrived in high society.

But, unlike many, the Schlossmann/Bondys were astute enough to see the writing on the wall. They decided to get out of Germany while there was still time and in 1936 father helped them to emigrate to England, where Herr Schlossmann obtained a position as a lecturer at a Cambridge college. Having sold their farm in Thansau – no doubt much below its market value – the Schlossmanns used the money to purchase the 'Hubertus' farm estate in the Northern Transvaal province of South Africa. This farm produced fast-growing eucalyptus trees, whose timber was used for pit props in the region's gold and iron-ore mines. The problem for the Schlossmanns was that the farm did not come with a resident manager. They were unqualified to do the job themselves, and did not have the time to go out and find someone suitable to fill the position.

The answer was right on their doorstep. Father's study of business administration, his time as manager of the Miesbach saw-mill, his fluent command of the English language, and his colonial days in Cameroon and German Southwest Africa before the Great War, made him the obvious candidate. Herr Schlossmann suggested that he take on the job of running the farm for two years, during which period he could find and train a suitable successor. Apparently father was all for it – even if it did mean leaving his family for a considerable length of time and later having to face the possible political consequences of offering support to Jews.

But all went smoothly. We children certainly didn't notice anything untoward. It wasn't until much later that I truly began to appreciate just how my parents must have been feeling during those two years and what conflicts of conscience they had no doubt had to suffer. Father wrote home regularly and his letters always arrived intact. Even local South African newspapers, sent quite openly as 'printed matter' and often containing political cartoons of a distinctly anti-German flavour, got through without being subject to any kind of control.

It was late in September 1937, midway through father's 'expedition' to darkest Africa, that I got my one and only close-up glimpse of Hitler – and not just Hitler, but Mussolini too. It happened at Kufstein railway station on the German-Austrian frontier, where Hitler was waiting to welcome the Italian dictator, who was coming to Munich on a state visit. Led by our French teacher Dr. Brünner – who, despite his inexplicable nickname of 'King Kong', was a gentle and understanding soul, much liked by us all – we were returning from a school trip to the Kaisergebirge mountains and, quite by chance, pulled in to Kufstein station at almost exactly the same time as the train carrying the Duce. Unexpectedly given a grandstand view of the reception ceremony, we spontaneously raised our right arms and bellowed "Heil Hitler" with youthful enthusiasm. I was only dimly aware that Dr. Brünner was not joining in the general euphoria. He neither extended his arm, nor did he utter a word.

Father's letters from the Transvaal, postmarked 'Politsi/Duivelskloof', continued to arrive with regularity. They were long chatty missives, full of interesting facts, and often mentioned the Messing family, who owned the farm adjoining the Schlossmann's Hubertus property. He was still in South Africa at the time of the Austrian Anschluss in March 1938 and wrote home approving wholeheartedly of the course Hitler had taken. In the summer holidays of that year two friends and I decided to make a cycle tour of Austria – or the 'Ostmark', as this recent addition to the Greater German Reich was now officially known.

From Rosenheim we pedalled our way through the Salzkammergut to Linz, where we hitched a ride aboard a Danube barge down to Vienna. From there it was over the Semmering to Graz, and thence via Klagenfurt, Villach, and Spittal – where we had to load our bikes on to a train for the trip through the Tauern tunnel – to Bad Gastein, Salzburg and back home to Rosenheim. At night we would either stay in youth hostels, or pitch our tents on farms where, without exception, we boarded for free. The whole tour cost me the princely sum of forty-seven Reichs-marks. From the people we spoke to we got the impression that the vast majority of Austrians had welcomed the Anschluss with Germany, but that many – maybe even most – would have pre-ferred it not to have been under Hitler.

Shortly before our cycle tour, in May 1938, mother had left for South Africa, where she planned to spend two months with father before they voyaged home together. During her stay out there the Messing family kindly showed my parents the local sights. Among my mother's most enduring memories were her visits to the Kruger National Park and the beaches of Mozam-bique.

My parents returned home at the time of the Munich Agree-ment, which ceded the Sudetenland territories of Czechoslova-kia to Germany. My father did not greet this latest development with as much enthusiasm as he had the Anschluss with Austria. And many people in Germany, especially those of the older gen-eration, shared his feelings. While they welcomed the move as a further repudiation of the still-open wound of the detested Treaty of Versailles, they were fearful of how the major European powers might react – "I hope this doesn't mean war", was a phrase that was often heard.

But when the Poles and the Hungarians also seized back the territories that they had lost to Czechoslovakia in 1919 without provoking the slightest military response from the west, it be-came clear that the Czechs had been left to their fate. We 'youngsters' were delighted at the turn of events. We fully shared the emotions of our teacher, Professor Ruckdeschel, as he stood in front of the class moved to tears of patriotic pride by the passages he was reading aloud from the *Völkischer Beobachter*.

If father had been ambivalent about the wisdom of Hitler's pushing through the Munich Agreement, an event that occurred just over a month later finally brought to an end his longstanding love-hate relationship with the Nazi Party. 'Kristallnacht', so called because of the sound of breaking glass, was an orchestrated assault on Jewish citizens and Jewish property throughout the Reich that took place on 9 November 1938. Although there was no open violence on the streets of Rosenheim, two burly SA party members stood outside the entrance of the town's only Jewish-owned shop, Westheimers the outfitters. They did not physically prevent anyone from going in, but ostentatiously noted the identity of those brave few who dared to do so.

Father was outraged when he learned what was happening. He immediately donned his uniform – he was by this time a Hauptmann in the reserves – went into town and marched straight into Westheimers. The two SA thugs were at a loss how to react. In the presence of an officer they had automatically stiffened to attention. But father's act of defiance had finally put him beyond the pale in the eyes of the party; he was already on the suspect list on account of our earlier close association with the Schlossmann family. Well aware of this, he addressed a thoroughly rude and disrespectful letter direct to the 'Brown House', the party's headquarters in Munich, cancelling his membership, stating that he had no wish to belong to a band of murderers!

But, like any old soldier worth his salt, father had made sure that his back was covered. One of his comrades from the Great War, Oskar von Ginkel, had elected to remain in the military. He had joined the small '100,000-man army' that the allies had permitted the Weimar government to maintain in the immediate post-war years, and had since risen to the rank of General and now commanded the Munich military base district. His office was responsible for the induction and placement of all conscripts and reserves in the Munich area. He quickly rushed through father's call-up to active service as a 'supplementary staff officer', at the same time promoting him to the rank of Major and appointing him to be his adjutant.

Father was thus safeguarded from any political reprisals, for during military service existing party membership automatically lapsed (likewise, no serving member of the armed forces could apply to join the party – an edict that remained in place until the attempt on Hitler's life by a group of army officers in July 1944). The Westheimers, by the way, later succeeded in emigrating to the United States. Their son had been in my class at school, but after the family's departure none of us ever heard a word from him again.

We may have been living in momentous times, but in that late autumn, early winter of 1938 all my attention was focussed on finally gaining those prized A and B gliding certificates. I had long ago mastered the take-off procedure: perching uncomfortably on the tiny seat of the Grunau G9, trying to peer past the wooden strut close in front of my face without going cross-eyed, while two of my comrades clung tightly to the tail of the glider and the rest charged off down the slope in two teams, pulling the wide 'vee' of the rubber bungee cord to the limit. At the shouted command "Release!" I no longer simply slid down the hill bumping and jolting on the 'skull-splitter's' single skid, but actually took to the air.

Papa Seitz coached me carefully for the A certificate, which required the pilot to fly a straight course for all of twenty seconds. He told me to keep my eyes firmly fixed on the tower of the church in the village below, and not to let myself be distracted by anything to left or right of that – especially that large steaming dung-heap in the farmyard at the foot of the hill. I must admit to being far too keyed up to remember much about those straightforward early hops that earned me the A certificate. But while practising for the more advanced B, which demanded that the glider be kept in the air for a full minute and that an S-course be flown, it was an absolute revelation to find myself being able to soar above the ground like a bird.

By the time I gained my B certificate our Grunau G9 had been fitted with an open plywood nacelle. Its aerodynamic benefit was minimal, but at least it offered some small psychological comfort to the pilot, who no longer had to stare down between his feet into nothingness. I also flew the Zögling 33, a basic glider very similar to the G9 but without the latter's notorious front strut, before progressing to the more advanced Grunau Baby early in 1939. I now had high hopes of attaining the C certificate, but at the end of 1938 father had dropped a bombshell. While in South Africa he had, as a precaution, made all the necessary arrangements with the local authorities for the entire family to move out there. We would be leaving for the Northern Transvaal in the spring.

In the event these plans came to naught. The rising tensions in Europe, culminating in the final dismemberment of Czechoslovakia in March 1939, had resulted in a blanket ban on emigration being imposed on all German citizens. We were caught in a trap. Personally, I wasn't all that sorry not to be going to South Africa. I wanted to join the Luftwaffe and become a fighter pilot. I had already been pre-programmed towards this end by my time in the Flieger-HJ. And of late my ambition had been given an added impetus by the sleek new Messerschmitt Me 109 fighters based at nearby Bad Aibling, which I saw almost daily as they climbed away over Rosenheim after take-off.

Father had no objection whatsoever to my volunteering for the armed forces – but did it *have* to be as a 'necktie soldier'? This was the derogatory term applied to the Luftwaffe, whose

Two women give the Nazi salute as they walk past the
martyrs' memorial on the side of the Feldherrnhalle building.
The author's father did his utmost to avoid this particular
corner of Munich.

uniform included a collar and tie, by members of the army, who still wore the traditional tunic buttoned high at the neck. As a dyed-in-the-wool infantryman – during the Great War he had served in the 11th Regensburg Infantry Regiment – father deplored such 'modern' innovations.

What he loathed above all else, however, was the raised arm 'Heil Hitler' salute used by members of the SA and SS. I can recall visiting him on one occasion, it must have been in the late spring of 1939, at his office in Munich's Seidlstrasse. Afterwards, in the street outside and much to the amusement of the passers-by, he proceeded to tear an enormous strip off a pair of unfortunate SS men who had had the effrontery to salute him with raised arms. Such was his profound dislike of this form of salute that, when in civilian clothes, he would always make a special point of walking down the narrow alley at the back of Munich's imposing Feldherrnhalle. This meant that he did not have to pass the memorial plaque commemorating those party members killed in Hitler's abortive putsch of 23 November 1923, which was affixed to the wall on the other side of the building. A permanent SS honour guard flanked this shrine to the movement's first martyrs, and everybody who walked past was expected to salute it. When in uniform father could, of course, put his hand to his cap in regular military fashion. But even this he tried to avoid as much as possible by taking the alternative route through the Viscardigasse.

And so the clouds darkened on the political horizon. For me and most of my peers they held the promise of adventure. Brought up on a steady diet of propaganda extolling the glorious exploits of past German history, our immature critical faculties were all too receptive to the ideas we were being fed. We dismissed the fears of our elders out of hand. We knew better.

Chapter 3

WAR IS DECLARED

The German invasion of Poland in the early hours of 1 September 1939 widened the gulf between the generations even more. Many people of my parents' age had watched Hitler's increasingly brazen expansionist foreign policies with mounting, if mostly unspoken, alarm. And when this latest venture – the first to be carried out by force of arms – resulted in England and France declaring war on Germany, they saw their worst fears realized. They remembered all too clearly the horrors of the First World War, which had ended in Germany's defeat little more than two decades ago. This renewed outbreak of hostilities witnessed none of the spontaneous popular jubilation that had greeted the start of the earlier conflict. It must be said, however, that the voices of the 'grumblers and grousers' – the party's own words – grew progressively fainter as the campaign in Poland ran its victorious course.

We of the younger generation viewed matters entirely differently. The final weeks' countdown to war had taken place during the summer holidays, which had given us ample time and opportunity to get together to follow and discuss the political developments with mounting patriotic fervour. Even after we had returned to school, the news from the front that September occupied our minds far more than did our studies. The unstoppable advance of our troops through Poland had totally captured our imaginations. Each new success was reported by a 'special announcement' on the radio. They were always preceded by a triumphant fanfare and were listened to with rapt attention.

It was our last year at school and we had been given automatic deferment from military service to allow us to take the Abitur, our final exams, which we were due to sit in the spring of 1940. But now something new had been introduced: the so-called 'War Abitur'. This did not involve any kind of examination, but was based entirely on a pupil's performance and his grades in school to date. If these were deemed to be satisfactory, the 'War Abitur' was duly awarded – provided the recipient volunteered for the armed forces when he turned eighteen.

To several of my school friends and myself this was hugely tempting. Filled with the true recklessness of youth, motivated by a mixture of allegiance to the fatherland and boredom with school, and fired up by visions of heroic deeds and impressive medals, it seemed to us to offer all the prospects of a great adventure. But such a course required parental consent. In those days the age of majority was still twenty-one. Resigned to the fact that they were not going to be able to stop me, my parents gave the necessary consent, albeit with a marked lack of enthusiasm. On the morning of my eighteenth birthday, 30 October 1939, I duly volunteered my services to the Luftwaffe.

A few days later I received my call-up papers ordering me to report to Manching airfield near Ingolstadt, some sixty kilometres to the north of Munich, on 15 November 1939. Manching was currently home to Fliegerausbildungsregiment 33 (Luftwaffe Basic Training Regiment 33) and it was here that I was to do my 'square-bashing'. Early on 15 November a small group of us – myself and four of my best friends from school – made our way to Rosenheim railway station fairly bursting with anticipation. Our mothers all turned up to see us off, of course, but tactfully kept their distance. They responded to our excited waves and laughing faces as the train pulled out of the station by fluttering their tear-stained handkerchiefs after us.

At Manching we were abruptly and unceremoniously plunged into the world of the military. But we had known what to expect and were not unduly alarmed. The barracks echoed to the sound of barking – not of the canine kind, but the shouted commands of the kapos, or NCOs, who were there to 'help' us draw our uniforms and equipment... "that helmet fits perfectly, it's your head that's the wrong shape!" As nothing else was available, I was issued with a tunic bearing a corporal's insignia. For the rest of the day, and much to my embarrass-ment, I was constantly being treated with unwarranted defer-ence and respect by people I didn't know. I couldn't wait to get back to our barracks room that evening and remove the of-fending braid.

After such a long passage of time it is difficult to remember much about my basic training, the main purpose of which seems to have been to teach us how to walk properly; some-thing we had apparently failed to master as civilians. My weeks at Manching are now just a blur of marching and drilling, drilling and marching. But one thing does stick in my mind. A misdemeanour by one resulted in collective punishment for all. I put my roommates' forbearance severely to the test on one occasion by arriving on morning parade without my rifle. Considering the importance attached to this item and the rev-erence in which it was held, the kapo's reaction can be imag-ined.

I could only catch the gist of what he was screaming at me in his near apoplectic fury, but I was led to understand, among other things, that nothing like this had happened in the German army since the days of Frederick the Great. The upshot was that we were all ordered to do fifty 'Prussians with applause' – fifty push-ups with a handclap between each. Another infringement of the rules (I wasn't the guilty party this time) resulted in a punishment that seemed to us to be less of a deterrent and more of a chance for the NCOs to relieve their boredom. The wrongdoer had to climb to the top of one of the tall pines that fringed our training ground. Swaying in the wind, he was then commanded to start shouting "cuckoo" at the top of his voice while the rest of us joined hands and danced around the base of the tree singing a well known ditty of the time, 'All the little birdies up there on high'.

In those early days of the war it was the norm for a Luftwaffe training base to house two units: one a basic training regiment such as ours, and the other an elementary flying training school. Both would share the same numerical designation and it was generally the case that a recruit, having successfully completed his basic military training in the first, would then progress to the second to commence flying training. But Manching's 'twinned' flying school, Sch/FAR 33, had been transferred up to Königsberg only days before we arrived and our regiment was moved lock, stock and barrel to join it there in early December.

Lying in the firing butts at Königsberg in the depths of an East Prussian winter, I came down with a nasty bout of influenza and found myself spending Christmas 1939 in the station sick quarters. At the beginning of January 1940 we were on the move again, this time along the coast to Elbing, close to the western end of the Frisches Haff lagoon. Here it was, if anything, even colder. In temperatures as low as minus 33 degrees there were several cases of frostbitten ears and noses. We were quartered in wooden barracks furnished with three-tier bunk beds. The huge iron stoves that were used to heat the rooms had to be fed throughout the night by the sentries coming on and off watch. The only trouble was that those in the lower bunks were constantly demanding more warmth while those in the top tiers – including me – were practically suffocating from the heat. We were only at Elbing for a month, thank God, before our basic training came to an end.

Early in February 1940 we four holders of the War Abitur, rather than being transferred across to the elementary flying training wing as we had hoped, unexpectedly found ourselves posted instead to a long-range reconnaissance Staffel. Equipped with Dornier Do 17s and based at Brüsterort on the extreme tip of the Samland peninsula northwest of Königsberg, this Staffel formed part of the Fernaufklärungsgruppe/Ob.d.L. which, as its designation suffix indicates, was a special unit subordinated directly to the Oberbefehlshaber der Luftwaffe (Luftwaffe High Command). Its present task was to fly reconnaissance missions along the Baltic to keep a covert eye on what the Russians were up to, even though the Soviet Union was signatory to a non-aggression pact with Germany at this time.

Despite our joining the Staffel as 'airmen/general-duties', in other words, the lowest of the low, the disappointment at not being selected for flying training was somewhat mitigated by the atmosphere that greeted us. Brüsterort was very much an operational station. There was none of the screaming of orders that had accompanied our every waking moment during basic training, nor any of the petty and seemingly pointless rules and regulations that had made our lives such a misery. Most of the Staffel's general-duties personnel were reservists and there was a very relaxed air about the place. We wouldn't have been unduly surprised had they addressed us as 'Herr' rather than 'Airman'.

Not that we behaved very much like Herren in our off-duty hours, which were spent larking about like the overgrown schoolboys we still were. In those early weeks of 1940 the winter landscape of the Baltic coastline was a magnificent natural spectacle. Before freezing over completely, the angry sea had hurled huge blocks of ice on to the beach. We scrambled and slid about on these like a pack of demented polar bears. Less enjoyable were the hours of backbreaking toil spent shovelling deep snow from the airfield's roads and runways.

In the spring of 1940 the Staffel was transferred from Brüsterort to Döberitz, west of Berlin. I was to remain with the unit until the late summer and so got ample opportunity to explore my country's capital city. As a Bavarian – and a provincial one at that – it made an enormous impression on me. To someone of my rather sheltered upbringing it all seemed so vibrant and modern. I was particularly struck by the Haus Vaterland, a so-called entertainment and pleasure venue on the Potsdamer Platz. This establishment even had a telephone on every table, which permitted you to strike up a conversation with a lady sitting anywhere in the room – something, I must admit, I never had the courage to do.

Towards the end of August 1940 I received a fresh posting. I was being sent to newly occupied France to join a mobile meteorological centre (Wetterzentrale XII mot.) currently based at Étampes, southwest of Paris. This move meant saying a final goodbye to my Rosenheim schoolmates. But at Étampes I soon found a new friend in Rudi Breu from Augsburg. Like me, he had chosen to take the War Abitur and was now serving as a deciphering clerk; our job being to decode the weather reports sent in by aircraft and ships out in the Atlantic, and by German-manned weather stations operating in Greenland.

A four-engined Focke-Wulf Fw 200 Condor maritime reconnaissance bomber of KG 40 based at Bordeaux. It was one of
the author's duties to decipher weather reports from aircraft
such as this flying far out over the Atlantic.

The unit was housed in a small country mansion on the
southern outskirts of Étampes. Our living quarters, we were
informed, were to be treated with the utmost respect and kept
in good order with the help of local cleaning ladies. I was given
a tiny room all to myself. It contained a small four-poster bed,
complete with canopy, and had presumably been the bedroom
of one of the daughters of the house. Unfortunately, it was also
an absolute flea trap. The place was alive with the things. In
fact, they were so numerous that during my first night, each
time I switched on the light to gain a few moments' respite
from their incessant biting, I swear I could clearly see the last
of my tormentors hurriedly jumping for cover! By the morning

I was so covered in bites that the CO of the unit, Dr.Christians, immediately called in the pest controllers to disinfect the whole house. After that there were no further problems.

Although he was our commanding officer, Dr. Christians was not, strictly speaking, a member of the Luftwaffe as such. A qualified meteorologist in his own right, his actual position was that of a Wehrmachtsbeamter, or official of the armed forces. I point this out because the met unit was a completely new experience for me. After the rigours of basic training, Brüsterort's relaxed atmosphere had been a welcome surprise. But it had nothing on Étampes. Here, although everyone was in uniform, things really were run on civilian lines. It was like working in a friendly office. There was none of the usual military hustle and bustle. If their badges of rank were anything to go by, the unit's wireless operators were all corporals. But they were like no corporals I had ever met; they were extremely pleasant and approachable. The cartographers who prepared the weather maps were themselves meteorologists and, like Dr. Christians, employed as officials of the armed forces.

The unit operated around the clock, working in three eight-hour shifts. Rudi and I asked to be put on the same shift and this request was readily granted. This meant that we could spend our off-duty hours together. Before our first venture out into occupied France we were told how we were expected to behave. We were not to strut around like conquering heroes, but to be polite and reserved. No attempts at personal contact with the French populace were to be made. We were only allowed out in groups of two or more, never alone, and only during the hours of daylight. After all, the war with France had only ended little more than two months earlier. For their part the French, while not openly hostile, were very cautious and guarded. Older people, in particular, remained extremely cold and brusque in their manner.

But Germany's behaviour towards occupied France began to pay dividends in a surprisingly short time. The official policy in these early days of not provoking confrontation, of trying to wean the French away from their mental alliance with the British and fostering better German-French understanding, certainly appeared to have an effect. It was not very long before we were able to move around in France pretty much as we would do at home. Rudi and I also found that our schoolboy French came in very handy. People's attitude became much more friendly at our stumbling attempts to address them in their own language.

Rudi was a huge fan of American swing music and I used to go along with him whenever he trawled through the record shops of Étampes looking to add to his collection of discs. These became increasingly hard to find, as many were now on the banned list for being 'un-German'. I can still vividly recall the dreamy expression of bliss on his face as he sat listening to his favourite melodies. Nobody in the unit, by the way, took the slightest offence at the illicit strains of 'Tiger Rag', 'Jeepers Creepers', 'Dinah' and the like, which regularly issued from Rudi's room.

Late in September 1940 the Wetterzentrale was transferred up to Deauville-Trouville at the mouth of the River Seine. These twin seaside resorts, famous as playgrounds of the rich in the years between the wars, lay along a kilometre of beach fronted by luxury villas and casinos. At the time of our arrival, however – still not all that long after the end of the war in France, and with the onset of autumn – the place had a somewhat deserted and melancholy air. We set up camp in one of the half-timbered, Norman-style villas overlooking the beach. The interior of the building was palatial, and the reason we had been allocated such grand quarters soon became apparent.

An even more imposing villa diagonally across from ours was the official residence of Generalfeldmarschall Hugo Sperrle, the AOC of Luftflotte 3, one of the two main air fleets currently engaged in the air war against England. The weather played an important part in the planning of operations and it was to be my and Rudi's duty, on alternate days, to deliver the latest met report to the great man's office. At first, I could hardly grasp the fact that I – an 'erk' of the lowest order – was to come into such close contact with one of the most important and powerful men in the Luftwaffe.

But my initial nervousness was soon dispelled by the frequency of my visits and by the Generalfeldmarschall's obvious interest in the information I brought to him. Besides, despite his intimidating appearance, he was known for the consideration he displayed towards the lower ranks, as I myself can testify. It was said that he reserved his worst tongue-lashings for the more senior members of his staff, something else I can vouch for – we could occasionally hear his roars of displeasure from the other side of the road.

Our present surroundings were even more attractive than those we had enjoyed at Étampes. The villa in which we were quartered was actually located in Deauville, where there was a quaint little fishing harbour. It was also a small but thriving regional market town offering a variety of diversions and amusements. In keeping with its recent cosmopolitan past, Deauville boasted a number of well-stocked music shops, which allowed Rudi to indulge his hobby to the full. Another sign of its previous international flavour were those villas still occupied by Americans living in France, most of which could be identified by the stars-and-stripes flying from the flagpoles in their front gardens.

One day Rudi and I happened to be passing one of these villas just as a couple of attractive American girls came out the front door. Rudi immediately started loudly to hum 'Jeepers Creepers', while I misguidedly tried to accompany him by whistling through my teeth. Total disaster! The looks that the two girls gave us were icy, bordering on the withering. We slunk away with our tails between our legs, trying to come to terms with the fact that we were not the two personable young gallants out for a pleasant afternoon's stroll that we had fondly imagined ourselves to be – just another pair of those 'nasty Nazis'.

It was an odd period of the war altogether. In the nine months between the defeat of France and the start of the Balkans campaign, most of continental Europe was in the grip of the same state of suspended animation that we were experiencing at Deauville. The only signs of military activity in our vicinity were the landing exercises being carried out along the Normandy coast not far from us. These were part of the preparations for the planned invasion of southern England. There may have been no fighting on the ground, but in the air – and at sea – it was a very different story.

The daylight phase of the Battle of Britain had peaked some weeks before. But the bizarre patterns of condensation trails, evidence of furious dogfights between the Luftwaffe and the RAF, were still sometimes to be seen in the skies above the Channel and over the Bay of the Seine. Occasionally, a formation of Me 109 fighters would swoop low along the beach in front of our villa. They made a thrilling sight, rekindling my burning ambition to be up there with them. But the wheels of Luftwaffe bureaucracy, it seemed, continued to grind exceeding slow.

Then, early in December 1940, the unit packed its bags and departed Deauville by truck for Villacoublay airfield on the southwestern outskirts of Paris. Our relaxed methods of working didn't alter one iota, but our surroundings took a definite nosedive in social terms. The Wetterzentrale occupied just one small corner of the large Villacoublay complex, which meant that we were suddenly thrust back into a totally military environment. For my part, the move wasn't entirely unwelcome. It had at least returned me to the world of flying machines – even if those machines were Heinkel He 111 bombers. At the start of the Battle of Britain, Villacoublay had housed all three Gruppen of Kampfgeschwader 55, the famous 'Greif', or 'Griffon' bomber wing.

Now, with the night blitz at its height, only the wing HQ and III. Gruppe remained. Although I had no direct contact with the crews of KG 55, if I was off-duty I would often watch the black-camouflaged Heinkels taking off into the night to attack a target somewhere in England. It was only a matter of days after our arrival at Villacoublay that I experienced for the first time the true reality of war. One of the heavily laden bombers suffered some sort of trouble and crashed on take-off. People rushed to the scene to help, but there was nothing that could be done. The four-man crew were burned beyond recognition. The horrific sight of their charred bodies, shrunken to the size of children, and the stench of burning fuel and roasted flesh made a lasting impression on me. It was a far cry from the heroic vision of air warfare that I had cherished for so long, but it did not weaken my resolve to fly.

Meanwhile, Rudi and I had all of Paris to explore. Clutching our street plans and historical guidebooks, we wandered through the city from one end to the other. The shock of the French defeat had long since worn off; life had returned and the streets were pulsating with activity, although petrol rationing meant that relatively few cars were to be seen on the roads. The armed forces' welfare organization even published a small booklet entitled *A German Guide to Paris*. Appearing monthly, this contained everything the visitor needed to know about the French capital – what was on in the theatre, the latest cinema releases, which cabarets to visit, where to shop, and much more.

There were also a number of 'Soldatenheime', or leave centres, where troops could spend the whole day if they so wished. Reichsmarschall Göring, who always made sure that nothing but the best was good enough for 'his' flyers, requisitioned one of the most sumptuous private residences in the city for this purpose. The Palais Rothschild was located in the exclusive Rue du Faubourg Saint-Honoré, close to the Place de la Concorde end of the Champs Elysées. Among its many attractions was the finest wine cellar in Paris, if not the whole of France, which the owner had been forced to abandon when he fled to England. The result was that even a nineteen-year-old wine philistine like myself was now able to pour a fine 1854 Haut-Sauterne down his throat for the princely sum of three-and-a-half Reichsmarks a bottle – an absolute steal. (In retrospect, the phrase 'throwing pearls before swine' springs rightly to mind.)

There was to be no home leave for Rudi and me over Christmas 1940, as the married members were understandably given priority. But we wanted to mark the occasion somehow, and so decided that on Christmas Eve we would climb to the top of the Eiffel Tower. The lifts were not working at this time, of course, but we tackled the stairs up to the second platform without too much difficulty. From there on, however, the going got tougher. The only way to ascend the final 150 metres to the top of the tower was via a steep and narrow circular metal staircase that wound itself tightly around the approximately one-and-a-half-metre diameter load-bearing central steel mast.

The higher we climbed, the giddier we felt. We made the mistake of looking down at the ant-like figures of the people on the ground far below, which only made things worse. Eventually we got to the top. At this height, very nearly 300 metres up, the swaying of the tower in the wind was very noticeable. This added to our general feeling of queasiness and unease, and we lost little time in setting off back down again. The climb up had taken us forty minutes. We made the descent in better time; at first keeping our eyes firmly fixed on the step immediately in front of us in order not to have to look straight down into the vertigo-inducing abyss yawning beneath our feet. But it was a marvellous experience all the same.

Almost from the start, the German authorities had been assiduous in their attempts to win over the people of Paris. Suitable German films, such as 'Hallo, Janine', were dubbed into French and drew long queues outside the city's cinemas. Another popular attraction was the concerts given by the Wehrmacht's military brass bands, which played selections from French and German operas and operettas in the parks and open spaces along the Champs Elysées and elsewhere. I was present at one of these concerts, held outside the Palais de Chaillot on the right bank of the Seine opposite the Eiffel Tower, where the German musicians ended their performance by striking up the 'Marseillaise'. The predominantly French audience broke into a spontaneous storm of delighted applause – a great number even raised their right arms to Hitler!

It mustn't be inferred from this, of course, that the French had suddenly developed a warm friendship for the Germans. As far as the majority of the population was concerned, it would be truer to say that the previous undercurrents of hostility were no longer present – or, at least, no longer apparent. In the shops we were served with civility. And requests for directions from strangers in the street were invariably answered politely.

But there was a darker side to life in Paris. Individual acts of terrorism were already being carried out against the German occupiers. They were admittedly few and far between at first, but this made their impact all the greater. I was witness to only one such atrocity. It was in the summer of 1941 and I was waiting for a train in a crowded metro station. Among the crush of people on the platform opposite were four girls in gaily-coloured summer frocks. Despite the general hubbub, I realized from the scraps of excited chatter I could hear that they were German, probably secretaries or typists working for one of the German firms that had set up offices in Paris. I waved across to them, indicating that they should move back from the edge of the platform. But they misunderstood my gestures and simply waved back laughing.

When the train drew in shortly afterwards, I could only watch in horror as the three or four men in civilian clothes who had been jostling and crowding round the girls suddenly pushed them on to the tracks in front of it. It was an absolute bloodbath. One of the young girls was screaming for her mother. But her cries gradually grew weaker until they finally ceased altogether. A few days later large red posters appeared on hoardings throughout the city announcing, in French, that – 'in accordance with the Hague Convention' – nine captive members of the resistance movement had been executed in retaliation for these cold-blooded murders. With the image of the slaughtered girls burned into my brain, I cannot deny feeling that justice had been done.

On 1 February 1941 I had been transferred from the Wetterzentrale to the Villacoublay permanent staff. Although I was still on the same base, my duties were entirely different – in fact, they were practically non-existent. My decoding work with the met unit had at least been of some value. But now that I was officially a member of the station company, I found myself with very little to do. The security of the operational side of the airfield was the responsibility of the resident KG 55, while the admin blocks and remaining areas were guarded by one of my new company's other platoons. As our off-duty hours now rarely coincided, I saw less and less of Rudi. We lost contact altogether after the invasion of Russia when he volunteered to serve in one of the Luftwaffe field battalions fighting on the eastern front, and sadly I never heard anything from him again.

As for me, my posting to the Villacoublay station company was clearly an attempt to make a 'proper' soldier out of me again before my nomination to officer cadet. I had never been endowed with a natural military bearing, and after eight months service in the relaxed atmosphere of the Wetterzentrale, any resemblance I may have had to an archetypal 'Defender of the Fatherland' was purely superficial. Determined, however, to fulfil my ambition of becoming a pilot, I pulled out all the stops to create the right impression.

This obviously had the desired effect, for it was not long before I was given the narrow strip of silver braid to wear on my right epaulette that identified me to all and sundry as an officer cadet. As my actual rank was still that of ordinary aircraftman, this made me something of an oddity. Another consequence of my newfound status was that I was required to dine in the officers' mess. I found this very daunting at first, but the station commander, an elderly Major and a fatherly type, took great pains to put me at my ease (incidentally, he also turned a benevolent blind eye to my increasingly ardent relationship with a pretty French girl working in station HQ.)

The station company's days were mostly taken up with exercises, target practice, route marches and sport. This was no doubt designed to hone us to the hardness of steel so that we would be ready and able to repulse any attack on the airfield by the wicked enemy – an event that, given the overall war situation at the time, seemed most unlikely to come to pass. One by-product of all this activity was my rise up the promotion ladder to the dizzying heights of aircraftman first class. But those in the corridors of power remained firmly of the opinion that I was still not yet enough of a soldier and that, furthermore, I needed to acquire at least some of the qualities of leadership.

The latter I could not argue with. And so, on 1 July 1941, I was despatched to attend a two-month NCOs' instructional course. This was held at Neukuhren on the Samland peninsula, less than twenty kilometres from Brüsterort, where I had first served with the long-range reconnaissance Staffel of the FAGr/Ob.d.L. early the previous year. But this beautiful stretch of East Prussian coastline presented a very different picture in the height of summer. The huge blocks of ice that I remembered had given way to long stretches of glorious sandy beaches. Not that we found much time for bathing. We were kept much too busy.

The main purpose of this course was to instil into ordinary young soldiers like ourselves the self-confidence that is fundamental to command. It took a lot of will power, not to say courage, to stand up in front of a sea of faces – some expectant, some obviously bored stiff, and a few clearly intent on causing trouble – and deliver a lecture to one's fellow course members. It was no easier out on the parade ground, where it was a favourite trick of the squad being drilled to keep marching straight ahead, preferably towards some obstacle or other, if the unfortunate pupil in temporary charge of them had not developed the necessary strength and clarity of voice to make himself properly understood over the distance – often rapidly increasing – that separated the two parties.

Sometimes, without warning and just to break the monotony, we would be sent out on a full day's route march. On one occasion we were rudely awoken from our slumbers at around three in the morning by the yells of the instructors sounding the alarm and ordering us to fall in outside in fifteen minutes in 'field marching order'. This meant being washed – shaving wasn't required – in full uniform, with a knapsack containing a day's rations, and clutching the 'soldier's best friend': our Karabiner 98k rifles. Such an order could only be carried out if our equipment was always kept to hand, in the right place and laid out in the regulation manner. This practice had been drummed into us during our basic training. In those dim and distant days we had dismissed it as yet another example of pointless military bullshit. But it was to prove its worth now, and we all somehow managed to scramble outside in time.

We set off along the dusty paths through the pinewoods skirting the coast, at first in columns, and then in open order. At intervals we had to take cover from imaginary enemy aircraft, or crawl through the trees on our stomachs, after which we would be ordered to proceed at the double 'just to loosen up the limbs'. At about 7am we were given an hour's break. But before eating breakfast we had to demonstrate that we still remembered how to construct two-man tents out of our groundsheets – another throwback to the days of basic training. A medic who had been trailing us by car also took this opportunity to treat the first of the morning's blisters.

And so it went on, and on – and on. The sun beat down. Despite being so close to the sea it was boiling hot. Hour succeeded weary hour and still we marched, crawled and doubled. I never knew East Prussia was so big. It was not until nearly 7pm that we finally arrived back in Neukuhren. We were led to a sort of mock-Bavarian beer garden, where the camp's brass band was waiting to serenade us. They did their best to revive our flagging spirits with a selection of popular tunes – but it was the free beer that really brought us back to life.

The two months spent at Neukuhren were the making of

me, even if you might not guess so today. This was down almost entirely to our course leader, Oberleutnant von Stein. He came from an aristocratic old East Prussian family, but displayed none of the high-handed militarism so often associated with his kind. He was strong on discipline – he needed to be to control a bunch of nineteen and twenty year olds like us – but his authority did not depend on his uniform and badges of rank. It was his personality that commanded obedience and respect. And this he passed down through the instructors to us budding NCOs.

We were given training that was undeniably hard, but it was also fair and focussed. At its end we were self-confident and able to think for ourselves. Had we remained in Oberleutnant von Stein's hands for much longer he would probably have forged us into some sort of élite unit. It is him I have to thank for setting me firmly on the last lap of the road towards my goal of becoming an officer and an operational pilot.

CHAPTER 4

THE START OF
MY FLYING CAREER

After completing the Neukuhren course I returned to duty with the station company at Villacoublay. Here, little had changed. But now that I had been promoted to Unteroffizier (corporal), I was put in charge of one of the sections responsible for airfield security. Our primary duties were to guard the main gates and other entrances to the base, and to patrol the perimeter. We worked in shifts with the other sections of the security platoon and so had plenty of free time on our hands. I spent most of my off-duty hours pursuing my love affair with Paris. Magical though these weeks were, I had few regrets when they were abruptly cut short by the news that I had finally been selected for flying training.

After passing the necessary medical examination – which entailed a lengthy rail journey to Halle, northwest of Leipzig – I was posted to Luftkriegsschule 4 at Fürstenfeldbruck near Munich. It was here, on 1 February 1942, that my officer training and flying career proper were to begin. My long cherished aim had at last been realized. I half suspected that my father, as adjutant to the General commanding the Munich base district, may have had a finger in the pie, especially in the choice of school (shades of Rosenheim grammar!), but I wasn't complaining.

The Luftkriegsschule, or air warfare school, had been built between the years 1936-1939. It was surrounded by pine forest, bordered to the south by the small town of Fürstenfeldbruck that gave the establishment its name, and to the north by the main Munich-Augsburg railway line. The school buildings were laid out in the form of an elongated U, one wing housing the classrooms, the other containing offices and living quarters. The open space between the two formed the parade ground – but the less said about that the better. Overall, the accommodation, the adjoining airfield and the numerous sports facilities represented state of the art technology.

The immediate environment was also very pleasant. Fürstenfeldbruck itself boasted several cafés and restaurants (although dancing in public places had unfortunately been banned since the start of the war with Russia in June 1941) and the local train service provided easy access to Munich – or the 'Capital of the Movement', as the city proudly liked to call itself during the days of the Third Reich – where a wide range of entertainments was on offer.

The one-year course, designed to get us our A and B military pilot's licences, which would qualify us to fly single and twin-engined machines up to a certain weight, began with eight weeks of theoretical studies. At its start I had been promoted to Fähnrich, or officer cadet, a rank roughly equivalent to midway between a corporal and sergeant. And so, in addition to the hours spent in the classroom, the school also embarked upon the process of turning my fellow course members and myself into officers and gentlemen. Part of the transformation involved teaching us how to dance (apparently a necessary social grace, but not something to be done in public!)

We were bussed into Munich for our dancing lessons, which were conducted by the legendary 'Peps' Valenci, who was the city's most distinguished dance teacher throughout the war and for many years afterwards. His lessons attracted only the cream of the cream. For a while one of my partners was a princess of the house of Wittelsbach. I hope I'm not being too ungallant when I say that the young lady's physical beauty was in inverse proportion to her nobility of birth, but she was a sweet and charming girl.

The sporting facilities within the school, which included a competition-sized swimming pool, were supplemented by sailing courses on the nearby Starnberger Lake. All in all, the state was investing a tidy sum in each and every one of us. But all too many would be called upon to pay a high price in return.

It was during this time that fate dealt our family a tragic blow with father's death on 15 March 1942. He had regularly suffered asthma attacks since being gassed in the trenches in the First World War. In the past he had always found temporary relief from the worst of these bouts by visiting the spa town of Bad Reichenhall for treatment. But on this occasion a particularly severe attack had struck him down in his Seidlstrasse office. He was unable to breathe and, despite being given an immediate antispasmodic injection, died of suffocation.

He was cremated in Munich's East Cemetery and his ashes were laid to rest in Rosenheim. In some ways I am glad that he did not have to live through the catastrophic years that lay ahead. Given his strong moral and political views, there is every chance that he may have become somehow involved with the army officers plotting to overthrow Hitler, which could have had dire consequences both for him and the family.

After two months of theoretical tuition, when we learned

A Focke-Wulf Fw 44 'Stieglitz' ('Goldfinch') primary trainer,
the type in which the author made his first powered flight.

about such things as the dynamics of flight and flying, the mechanics of aircraft and aero engines, air navigation, radio procedures, air and ground tactics and the like, the great day finally dawned: 24 April 1942 – my first powered flight! Out on the apron we eight pupils clustered round our sergeant-pilot instructor, hanging on his every word as he briefed us on the first of the three familiarization flights he would be giving each of us.

He began at the very beginning: how to get into the aircraft. Never, ever, tread on any fabric surface. Place your left hand on the front edge of the cockpit sill, support yourself with your right hand on the rear edge, draw up your legs and – without stepping on the seat – slide your feet under the instrument panel and on to the rudder pedals. When my turn came I followed these instructions to the letter. As the pupil, I occupied the front cockpit. Sitting there, waiting for the mechanic to swing the propeller into life, I was so keyed up with excitement that I very nearly took to the air before the machine did.

The propeller started to turn, the engine caught, the mechanic removed the chocks from the wheels and jumped quickly out of the way. Now came the big moment. The throttle at my side slid forward as the instructor in the rear cockpit smoothly increased power. The Focke-Wulf Fw 44 Stieglitz – registration CA+GG – bumped across the grass quickly picking up speed. The tail lifted and we rose into the air climbing steadily. The thirty-two-minute flight passed in a flash – a kaleidoscope of sights, senses and emotions. The two-and-a-half-year wait was at last behind me. It had all been worthwhile. Now all that mattered were the flying hours going into my logbook.

And those hours soon began to mount up. Early in July 1942 our course was moved out to the school's satellite field at Bad Wörishofen. This small station was set in picturesque countryside about fifty kilometres WSW of Fürstenfeldbruck. The buildings were all of wooden construction and there was an altogether informal and relaxed – in fact, almost civilian – air about the place. It was here on 15 July 1942, after forty-five flights with the instructor literally looking over my shoulder, that I first went solo. I lifted off in Stieglitz PF+UT at exactly 10.36hrs. One careful circuit and I brought her gently back down to earth again at 10.40hrs. Although flight number forty-six may have lasted only four minutes, it was entered into my logbook with a real sense of achievement. Another hurdle cleared in my ambition to become a fighter pilot.

Three days later I was promoted to Oberfähnrich, or officer aspirant. This rank was the first real rung on the ladder to becoming an officer, without the holder actually being commissioned. It was a sort of hierarchical no-man's land: on the one hand, an Oberfähnrich could no longer be called upon to perform tasks such as 'duty NCO' but, on the other, he was not yet qualified to carry out an officer's responsibilities. It meant, in effect, that I was required to do nothing except concentrate on my flying. On reflection, that is not strictly accurate. In their wisdom, the authorities had decided that we were not just learning to be pilots. We also needed to be reminded that we were soldiers too – soldiers who, if the worst came to the worst, would be capable of defending their airfield from enemy attack. And so a series of field exercises was organized.

There was only one flaw. The fifty kilometres or so that separated Bad Wörishofen from Fürstenfeldbruck also meant that we were that far removed from the eagle eye of the school commander, Generalmajor Sonnenberg, and his disciplinary watchdogs. The result was that the exercises quickly developed into a riotous game with everyone hurling thunderflashes about with abandon. The climax came when our arch mischiefmaker, one Materleitner, smuggled one of these very noisy but harmless devices back into camp and dropped it down a latrine.

The thunderflash exploded with a tremendous 'whoomph' and the occupants of the latrine hut – five stalls a side; what we called a 'ten-cylinder' job – emerged with their trousers round their knees and their backsides liberally bespattered with the fruits of many previous visitors' labours. "They're bombing the shithouse!" somebody yelled in panic. Everyone stared up into the clear blue sky, some less innocently than others, but there wasn't a single enemy aircraft to be seen.

Such episodes aside, our flying training continued uninterrupted as we gradually developed our newly acquired skills, were taught new ones, and were introduced to other aircraft types. We had already been shown how to respond to various emergencies – what to do in the event of a stall, for example – prior to going solo. Next came what were known as small, better described as local orientation flights.

These consisted of the instructor tooling around in the general vicinity of the field while the pupil marked the course the aircraft was following on the flight map strapped to his thigh. It was a perfect summer's day with excellent all-round visibility when my turn came to climb into the front seat of the Focke-Wulf. Convinced that this was going to be a piece of cake, I relaxed in the warmth of the sun as I casually jotted down the first orientation points that showed we were heading WSW into the picturesque Allgäu region.

After a little while, however, doubts began to creep in. Was that lake coming up on the left – the one with the wood on one side and the road junction on the other – really the same as the one shown on my map? Despite our slow speed, the landscape below was hurtling past far too quickly as I desperately searched for some sort of landmark to fix our position. And then, when the instructor unkindly threw in a few extra turns for good measure, I was well and truly lost. Luckily, a few minutes later I was able to pinpoint exactly where we were... or where I *thought* we were. After landing I confidently showed the instructor my map marked with the route we had taken. I was promptly disabused. We had indeed flown over the Allgäu, but not along the course I had plotted. At first I flatly refused to believe this, pointing out that facts shouldn't always be taken at face value; I even had the temerity to suggest that the map might be wrong.

Various expressions chased each other across the instructor's face. He finally settled for foaming rage, and than proceeded to give me an almighty rocket, not forgetting to trot out the phrase that I was beginning to think was obligatory for any

NCO in a fury – the one about 'not since the days of Frederick
the Great...' As a punishment I was ordered to run along beside
the Focke-Wulf as the instructor taxied it back to dispersal;
not a pleasant experience in the baking heat and with the seat-
pack parachute bumping against the backs of my knees the
whole way.

But it was a lesson well learned. Never again did I set out
on an overland flight without giving it my full attention. The
next such exercise was a straightforward hop from Bad Wörishofen to Fürstenfeldbruck and back. The two stages went
into my logbook as flights forty-nine and fifty. They were made
in Fw 44 PF+UT, the machine in which I had first soloed, and
took just forty minutes. Later I would start to venture further
afield to such destinations as Roth near Nuremberg, Wels in
Austria, Strasbourg and Vienna.

It was in DB+CO that I was introduced to the 'slip', the
steady banking turn made just before touching down. One of
the objects of the slip was to shorten the landing approach.
During the manoeuvre the pilot was able to look down sideways at the ground sliding past not far below. But, inexplicably,
we had great difficulty at first in mastering the art of the slip.
We would invariably start to bank far too soon – over the
grounds of the local spa hotel, in fact. To be even more precise,
right over that secluded part of the grounds reserved for the
lady guests who wished to indulge their passion for nude sun-
bathing. Sadly, the strident protests of the hotel management
soon put a stop to our fun and games, and the slip became just
another item to add to our growing repertoire.

As part of the preparations for our overland, or cross-country, flights we had also been shown how to carry out 'precision'
landings. The instructor would switch the engine to idle at an
altitude of about 1,200 metres somewhere close to the field
and we would then have to put the machine down as close to

58

the landing cross as possible. This was to give us the confidence to make a deadstick landing should we suffer engine failure in the middle of a cross-country. To the same end, it was also drummed into us that we must always keep a close eye on the passing terrain and make a mental note of all suitable emergency landing sites along our route.

I made nine consecutive flights, mostly in Fw 44 BO+CH, practising precision landings. The next, number ninety, saw me go up for the first time in the Bücker Bü 131 Jungmann. This was a two-seater biplane very similar to the Fw 44 in speed and performance, and the four-minute circuit that constituted my familiarization flight on the type posed no problems. And it was in another Bü 131, DB+GE, that I was taught how to perform a steep turn. This, however, took a lot more getting used to. For during such a manoeuvre the elevators and the rudder appear to exchange roles.

They have not actually done so, of course: they are still moving the aircraft in the same direction relative to itself. But when in a steep bank, it is the elevators that govern the direction of flight and the rudder that has to be employed to make the machine climb or dive. After wrestling long and hard with this, it was almost a relief to climb back into an Fw 44 (BB+EM) for flight number 154: my first solo cross-country. By this time – it was now August – we had been recalled to Fürstenfeldbruck, and the 120-kilometre flight from there to Roth took me exactly sixty-seven minutes.

The trip to Roth had gone like clockwork. But another cross-country the following month – to Crailsheim in Bü 131 BA+WT – was a different matter. Foolishly, I ignored the warning that we had been given in the classroom never to fly with a head cold. The climb to my cruise altitude of 800 metres was trouble-free. But when I started to let down on approaching Crailsheim a piercing, agonizing pain immediately lanced from my left ear, through my head and into the back of my neck. I quickly regained the twenty-thirty metres of height that I had already lost and began to circle, wondering what on earth to do next. But there was no option. I would have to land sooner or later. Very cautiously, keeping my rate of descent to an absolute minimum so that the pain was just about bearable, I started to come down. When I finally landed some fifteen minutes later, the staff at Crailsheim naturally wanted to know what the problem was. After I had explained, the duty MO was summoned. He unblocked my ear passages and all was well.

We had been transferred back to Fürstenfeldbruck (or 'F Bruck' as it was then commonly called; today's 'Fürsty'-ites' please take note!) in order to be given tuition on some of the other aircraft types operated by the school. These included the Arado Ar 66 biplane, the Klemm Kl 35, a two-seater low-wing monoplane originally designed for private ownership, and the Bücker Bü 181 Bestmann, another monoplane initially intended for sports flying, but with an enclosed cabin seating two side-by-side. We flew numerous training circuits in each of these machines, none lasting much more than five minutes. But in recompense for our enforced return to F Bruck with its stricter rules and more military regime, we also began to practise close formation flying. This demanded the utmost concentration, but proved to be great fun.

Then, late in September, we were sent back to the freedom of Bad Wörishofen to begin the most interesting part of the whole course: aerobatic flying. On 28 September we were each taken up for a thirty-minute demonstration flight –in my case in Fw 44 BO+EI – before getting down to practice in earnest. The programme we would be required to fly to prove our proficiency consisted of a climb to 1,500 metres, slow roll to left, dive full throttle into a loop, half loop to right, half roll recovery to left, and land.

THE START OF MY FLYING CAREER

The entire sequence had to be flown in a straight line, and a stretch of railway track that carved arrow-straight through the countryside nearby was to prove an invaluable aid in helping us keep our bearings as we gradually mastered the required figures. The instructors paid particular attention to the loop, which had to form a perfect circle in the sky – woe betide anyone who 'laid an aerial egg'!

After our first ten aerobatic practice flights we transitioned to the Focke-Wulf Fw 56 Stösser, a single-seat high-wing monoplane advanced trainer. Fully aerobatic, it was an absolute joy to fly, as I discovered for myself the moment I lifted off in TN+HL for my first brief familiarization hop. Although light and responsive, the Stösser – or Sparrow Hawk – was also exceptionally sturdy. It was rumoured that the manufacturer was actually offering a cash prize to any pilot who could make the machine's parasol wing part company with the fuselage while in a dive.

We needed no further urging. But, despite all our best efforts, the Focke-Wulf company's finances remained intact – and fortunately so did we. Just to be on the safe side, I first climbed to an altitude of 4,000 metres before tipping the Fw 56 into a near vertical dive. Standing upright on the rudder pedals, I reached a speed of nearly 450km/h before having to pull out. The engine was screaming like a banshee the whole time, making enough noise to waken the dead. It certainly upset the local populace. Somewhat thoughtlessly, we had been conducting our trials over the town. And this proved too much even for the worthy citizens and hotel guests of Bad Wörishofen, who were usually remarkably tolerant of our antics. Strong protests were voiced and an official complaint was lodged by the Bürgermeister. As a result we were forced to conduct our operations over the open land some kilometres to the east of town.

Aerobatic training did not occupy all our time. During October, in addition to a number of cross-countries – some flown in formation – we were also introduced to night flying. This caused some apprehension at first, but once we began to get the hang of it, we discovered that flying in darkness had a special appeal all of its own. On 1 November 1942 I was promoted to Leutnant (although this was not made substantive until 3 January 1943). Three days later I celebrated my commission by making my first night solo: flight number 293 in Arado Ar 66 BO+DN.

During our night flying the field's perimeter lights were kept on for take-offs and landings. This was to enable the pupil to judge his position and height. And the runway itself was illuminated immediately prior to touchdown. But in between these times the trainee pilot was very much on his own. As it was now November the nights were dark and the skies were generally overcast. Once aloft, however, a few glimmers of light could always be seen despite the stringent blackout regulations, and there was just enough residual visibility left to distinguish the dim outline of the horizon. Swaying gently, an occasional small shower of sparks spraying from its exhaust, the easy-going Arado purred along contentedly. I completed two circuits without any fuss or bother and another ten minutes of flying time were added to my logbook.

But the highlight of the course, as far as I was concerned, was the aerobatics test. I took this on 11 November – quite by chance, it happened to be my 300th flight – and I managed to achieve eight out of the nine possible marks awarded. We had already been questioned as to which branch of the flying arm we wanted to join. My reply, of course, had been fighters. And I hoped that this performance would boost my chances and help get me the posting of my choice.

In the final weeks of our training we became acquainted

with two other aircraft. The Arado Ar 96 advanced trainer was a modern all-metal monoplane in which the pupil and instructor sat in tandem beneath a long glazed canopy. In contrast, the Heinkel He 51 was a rugged, single-seat open cockpit biplane that had been the Luftwaffe's first standard fighter back in the mid-'thirties. Another difference between the two machines was that the Arado had a retractable undercarriage. This was a refinement we had not encountered before – and it was very nearly my undoing. Like a complete idiot, I accepted a bet that I couldn't retract the Arado's wheels during take-off while still on the ground.

Luckily, I somehow managed it; judging the exact moment and pulling up the undercarriage just as the machine was on the very point of lifting off. For a split second it tipped to the right as the mainwheel on that side began to retract a fraction before the left-hand one. Then I was safely up and away. It was all over in a flash, but my action had not escaped the notice of the instructors, who kicked up the devil of a fuss. I will forever be grateful that they very sportingly decided to keep the matter to themselves. Otherwise I would have been well and truly for it under Para. 92 of the Luftwaffe disciplinary code, subsection 'endangering life and machine'.

On 13 January 1943 I took off from Fürstenfeldbruck for the last time – and in the regulation manner, I hasten to add. During my ten months' flying training at the air warfare school I had made 354 flights, racking up a total of some 103 flying hours. As at the end of every course, there followed a general parting of the ways. I was subsequently to meet up with only two of my fellow F Bruck pupils again when Leutnant Otto Wania, Oberfähnrich Peter Ullmann and I all served together in 4./JG 2 'Richthofen'. Sadly, both came to tragic ends. Otto, although himself born in Czechoslovakia, was murdered by vengeful Czechs at the end of the war. Peter died from burns suffered in a fire at his Munich home in 1966.

But the strongest bond of friendship that I forged at LKS 4 was with my regular instructor, Feldwebel Maurer. We were to remain in touch well into the post-war years. It was then he told me that he had still been flying the Fw 44 Stieglitz right up until the end of hostilities. During those final weeks, however, he was no longer instructing – his machine had been crudely armed with machine guns and he was carrying out low-level attacks on American troops advancing on Munich.

CHAPTER 5

TRAINING TO BE A FIGHTER PILOT

After successfully completing the course at Fürstenfeldbruck, we were all given our next postings. I was delighted to find that my application to join the fighter arm had been approved. I had half-hoped to be sent to the fighter school at St. Raphael on France's Côte d'Azur, but was more than content to settle for JG 107 based at Nancy-Essay in eastern France instead. As it turned out, the eight months I spent at Nancy were to be the happiest of my entire flying career.

JG 107 was a fighter training Geschwader comprising just one Gruppe. It had been brought into being less than a week prior to my arriving at Nancy, created by the simple expedient of redesignating the previously resident Jagdfliegerschule 7. I was introduced to the harsh realities of life at a fighter-training unit on my very first day. It was 1 February 1943 and I was eating lunch in the officers' mess when there was the dull thump of an explosion outside. An Me 109D had spun in while approaching to land. This fatal accident had personal consequences for me. As the newest arrival, I was detailed to

65

command the guard of honour at our late comrade's burial in Nancy cemetery. I am sad to say that this was not an isolated incident. By the time I left Nancy on 1 October, six more of the school's trainees had been laid to rest with full military honours.

But before beginning my fighter training proper, I was given the opportunity to enjoy an unexpected spot of leave. I had my Bavarian nationality to thank for my good fortune. Some ancient dictionaries defined Bavarians as 'native mountain folk'. It was assumed from this – not altogether wrongly – that I therefore had to be an experienced mountain skier. And so a few days after my arrival at Nancy I was on the move again. This time I had been ordered to take a group of ten men to the Geschwader's alpine ski chalet at Zug near Lech, high in the Arlberg Pass, where the weather was to remain perfect throughout the whole of our two weeks' stay.

The day's duties began – not too early, it goes without saying – with morning parade, after which I gave skiing lessons just like any civilian instructor would. These continued after lunch and occupied the rest of the afternoon. Unlike morning parade, the evening meal was taken early – again for obvious reasons: it gave the men that much more time to explore the delights, both natural and physical, of the nearby ski resorts of Lech and Zürs.

One of the unit's mess cooks had accompanied us and so the inner man was also well catered for. Together with his pots and pans, he had brought along with him half a wild boar, compliments of our Gruppenkommandeur, Hauptmann Franz Hörnig, who was a keen huntsman and had bagged this particular specimen during one of his frequent hunting expeditions into the woods of the Lorraine.

Although they were undoubtedly enormous fun, there was also a more serious side to these organized skiing trips. The reason behind JG 107 having its own chalet in the Austrian Alps lay in the belief that the sport of skiing demanded split-second reactions, a quality essential in a successful fighter pilot and one to be developed by any and every means possible. But despite this semi-official side to our 'holiday', I was permitted to invite my mother to join us at the chalet for the last few days. She enjoyed her brief stay immensely. But then, on the day of our departure, the weather finally broke. Snow fell heavily and we had to make our way down to the local railway station packed together like sardines on two horse-drawn sleighs.

This proved altogether too uncomfortable for mother, who declared that she would rather take her chances on the small toboggan we had with us. This was duly tied to the back of the second sleigh with a lengthy piece of rope and off we set again. Some little while later I was startled to hear one of the men shouting, "Herr Leutnant, we've lost Mama!" (I always addressed, and referred to my mother as 'Mama'). I peered behind me and, sure enough, there was the empty toboggan weaving about from side to side, but not a sign of mother. She must have fallen off. Several of us immediately set off back up the track to look for her. Luckily, the mishap must have only just occurred, for we soon caught sight of her, clearly none the worse for her ordeal, as she appeared out of the driving snow calling and waving energetically.

Refreshed and reinvigorated by two weeks of mountain air, I finally got down to the serious business of fighter training. At Nancy I had been assigned to 3./JG 107. This Staffel was commanded by Hauptmann Adalbert Sommer, a fifty-victory ace who had previously served as Staffelkapitän of 7./JG 52 on the eastern front, where he had been awarded the German Cross in Gold. Initially I found myself carrying on from where I had left off at Fürstenfeldbruck by flying standard trainer types. Later I would progress on to real fighters. The big difference was that at F Bruck we had been taught to fly, whereas at Nancy, under

Sommer's supervision, we would be taught to fly *operationally* – in other words, we were there to learn the tactics used in fighter combat.

We began by mastering the art of flying in pairs. The Rotte, or pair, was the smallest tactical formation employed by the Luftwaffe's fighter arm. During our training sessions the instructor would take the part of the Rotte leader, while the trainee flew as his wingman (or 'Katschmarek', to use the peculiar Luftwaffe jargon of the time.) In combat formation the two machines were required to fly at exactly the same level and about fifty metres apart. Due to the restricted rearward visibility in a frontline fighter aircraft, no pilot was permitted to fly a combat mission on his own.

The Rotte formation allowed each man to cover the other's back. This is why it was absolutely essential for the wingman always to remain level with his leader and not to lag behind. Even in straight flight this was not as easy as it sounds. And during a change of course it was downright difficult. For then the wingman would immediately have to cut either behind or above his leader in order to maintain correct station.

Training flights spent practising the Rotte formation usually lasted about an hour, with the final five minutes almost invariably being devoted to a 'Karussell', or 'merry-go-round'. This was when the instructor would pull ahead and start to fling his machine about all over the sky. It was the pupil's job not just to stay on his tail, but also to try to manoeuvre into a good firing position. Again, this seemed simple enough when demonstrated on the ground with the aid of models. But trying to get – and keep – a twisting, weaving machine in your sights when in the air was a different matter entirely. The ideal firing position, directly astern of an opponent who was holding to a steady course in front of you and sitting squarely in your gunsight, hardly ever occurred in real life. Very few enemy fighter pilots were obliging, or dim enough to fly straight and level in hostile airspace.

This is why such great importance was placed on our Karussell sessions. Firstly, they got the trainee pilot accustomed to judging distance and space relative to his target, and thus how much angle of deflection, or lead was required – in other words, how far ahead of his opponent he needed to aim – in order to score a hit. Secondly, in particularly steep turns the instructor's machine could easily be obscured momentarily by the engine cowling of the pupil's own aircraft and then be lost altogether. The Karussell was a way of teaching the trainee to fly 'by the seat of his pants' and not risk losing sight of his opponent by continually glancing down at his instruments. The golden rule was always to fly smoothly – any untidy or skidding turns meant increased drag and thus an inevitable reduction in performance.

But smooth flying alone did not automatically guarantee victory in aerial combat. We were also taught two rather unorthodox manoeuvres that could help us gain a decisive advantage over our opponent. One of these, I've already mentioned, the slip – taken over directly from the English – was a fairly straightforward affair. It entailed the use of the rudder alone to make the aircraft slip, or crab sideways. The stick and ailerons were not touched, so there were no outward signs of a turn. The theory was that, although the machine *appeared* to be holding its course, it was actually sliding to one side out of the line of fire of an enemy attacker.

The other manoeuvre was more violent and potentially more dangerous, involving as it did the deliberate disruption of the airflow over the wing surfaces. The Gerissene Kurve (crafty turn), as it was known to us, was, in fact, a turn with full ninety-degree bank. If there was an enemy machine on your tail this could get you out of a tight corner and, if executed properly, could quickly transform you from the hunted into the hunter.

The procedure was as follows: chop the throttle to kill speed, at the same time full rudder and stick in the desired direction – say to the left – in order to stand the machine on its wingtip in a slightly nose-up attitude, then immediately start to dump flap in measured doses to reduce the angle of attack.

By this stage the aircraft has practically turned on its heel and instantaneous – but smoothly applied – full throttle is now required so that, for a split second, the machine is quite literally hanging on its screw. If a stall is to be avoided, it is at this precise moment that the aircraft has to be returned to normal flight attitude by pushing the stick slightly forward and retracting the flaps to increase the airspeed. As can be imagined, the Gerissene Kurve called for great delicacy of touch and took a lot of learning.

But, in the course of numerous mock combats, learn it we did. Perhaps unsurprisingly, these sessions also brought home to us the fact that, in a classic dogfight between two equally matched aircraft, the pilot who stood the greater chance of winning was the one who executed the smoothest manoeuvres and displayed the better mastery of his machine.

The next stage of our training saw us flying in Schwarm formation. The Schwarm was one step up from the Rotte and consisted of four aircraft made up of two pairs, each comprising a leader and a wingman. The process of changing course when operating as a Schwarm demanded even greater concentration from the two wingmen as they cut behind and above their respective leaders. The movement was akin to a brief aerial ballet and resulted in the Schwarm flying on a new heading, but in a mirror image of its previous formation.

Each lesson spent carefully practising these set moves would then, as usual, end in a heady five-minute Karussell. In addition to aerobatics and orientation flights, the training programme now also included gunnery practice firing at ground targets. Our flying was still being done mainly on the Arado Ar 96, but we also made use of the Fw 56 Stösser on the firing ranges.

The first anniversary of my father's death – 15 March 1943 – occurred during this period. As the airspace in which we did much of our training happened to extend northwestwards from Nancy along the line of the River Meuse, I took the opportunity to make an orientation flight in an Ar 96 on this date. Once aloft, orientation turned into commemoration as I followed the course of the Meuse northwards from St. Mihiel to Verdun. For it was in this area, among many others, that father had fought during World War I when he and his company had captured the Camp des Romains fortress on the east bank of the river in the autumn of 1914.

It must have been around this time too that Franz Brosius, who had been a fellow pupil of mine at the air warfare school and, like me, had been posted here to JG 107, met a particularly tragic end. We were both scheduled for aerobatics in an Fw 56 and had to decide who was to go up first. As it was rather a cold day and I was only wearing ordinary shoes, I suggested that he take the first stint while I went to fetch my fur-lined flying boots.

As I gave him a hand to strap himself in, I reminded him to make sure that the safety hook behind the central lock of his parachute harness was pushed fully home. While making my way back to my quarters I glanced up now and again to watch his performance. As he pulled out of a left-hand turn, I was horrified to see him roll over the edge of the cockpit and fall out of his parachute. It was a truly awful thing to witness. The Focke-Wulf bored into the earth in a near-vertical dive and I saw Franz hit the ground not far away from it.

We raced to the spot and were confronted by a gruesome sight. Franz lay on his back; both arms dislocated and distorted, his lifeless eyes wide open, and his flight overalls and tunic ripped apart from top to bottom. He must have been thrown

71

The Luftwaffe flew a number of captured Spitfires.
This is believed to be a photo-reconnaissance version
that forced-landed in Holland. The author found the
British fighter's cockpit 'too roomy' after the snug confines
of the Me 109.

back into the air by the force of the initial impact, for there was
a twenty-centimetre deep depression in the soft soil right next
to him. The skin of his face looked as if it had been singed.

Subsequent investigation established that this had been
caused by a small explosion on board the aircraft, although there
were no signs of a fire. It was also found that the vital safety
hook had *not* been secured properly. When Franz had thrown
himself out of the cockpit, his parachute harness had come undone. His death, the enquiry concluded, had been brought

about solely as a result of his own negligence.

On 2 May 1943, three months into my time at Nancy, I finally got my hands on a Messerschmitt Me 109. Admittedly, it was only a Dora, the obsolete and relatively unsophisticated Me 109D variant with a 700hp Junkers Jumo 210 liquid-cooled engine, but even this early example of the type was an absolute revelation. Just to sit in its cockpit, which seemed sculpted to accommodate the human form with not a centimetre of superfluous space to spare, to look out through that tiny windscreen over the impossibly long engine cowling, gave the pilot the feeling of being at one with the aircraft – that man and machine were a single lethal organic entity.

The only weak point in the design of the Me 109 – and this afflicted not just the Dora, but every other variant of the breed as well – was the spindly, knock-kneed undercarriage. Take-offs and landings, the latter in particular, called for the utmost concentration on the part of the pilot. When speed was reduced after touchdown, the Me 109 showed a marked tendency to swing to the left due to the reverse torque of the propeller. If the pilot did not act in time to correct this swing, it could all too easily develop into a fully blown ground loop, which invariably resulted in the undercarriage legs being sheared off.

Take-offs presented slightly less of a problem. The answer was to do a 'tail-dragger'. If all three wheels were kept on the ground for as long as possible, the combined effect of the tail-wheel and the increasing pressure of the slipstream on the rudder were enough to compensate for the torque effect. But the pilot then had to display a fine sense of judgement for the feel of the aircraft as it lifted off. Torque could also prove deadly if the pilot had the misfortune to overshoot on landing. If he was trying to go round again, but shoved the throttle forward too abruptly while the aircraft was hanging in the air, its speed too low and with insufficient lift, the sudden torque could flip the machine over onto its back – almost always with fatal consequences for the unfortunate occupant.

But once these foibles had been explained to us and accorded their due respect, the Me 109 proved an absolute joy to fly. It was light on the controls and extremely responsive. The only exception was in a fast dive, when the stick had to be kept pushed fully forward. This required a considerable amount of brute force. The pupil pilot was also strongly advised not to exceed the machine's stability limit – the point at which he could expect to see the wings part company with the rest of the airframe and wrap themselves round his ears!

After the Dora we progressed first to the Me 109E Emil, which was powered by a 1,100hp Daimler-Benz DB 601A, and then on to the more aerodynamically refined Me 109F Friedrich with its uprated DB 601E, before finally being entrusted with the Me 109G Gustav. This latter, powered by a 1,500hp DB 605 engine, was, at that time, the latest variant of Professor Messerschmitt's famous design and currently the Luftwaffe's standard front-line fighter. We at JG 107 had been presented with a grand total of two Gustavs.

As well as being used for training purposes, this prized pair had to be kept at operational readiness in case there was an emergency scramble. For by now, as well as the occasional RAF reconnaissance Mosquito passing by high overhead, allied Jabos, or fighter-bombers, were beginning to poke their noses down towards our corner of France. This gave added impetus to our air-to-air gunnery practice. But not once did an enemy aircraft deign to show itself in front of our Revi gunsights.

And so we continued to revel unmolested in the freedom of the early summer skies, throwing our machines about with still youthful abandon and indulging in exciting games of chase against a backdrop of majestic and ever-changing cloudscapes. I remember on one occasion flying between two enormous cumulus clouds and finding myself above a field of pristine white, some 100 metres across and 500 metres long, which sloped gently upwards to end in a magnificent celestial arch where the two clouds met and intertwined. I could not resist the temptation to perform a slow roll just above the floor of this aerial valley before exiting through the arch and pulling into a steep turn through the clear cobalt sky that surrounded the whole mighty edifice.

In addition to the Me 109, the two Staffeln of JG 107 based at Nancy – 2./JG 107 operated separately out of Toul just over twenty-five kilometres to the west of us – also had several foreign aircraft on strength for training sessions. These were mostly ex-French air force machines, including two fighter types, the radial-engined Bloch 151 and the liquid-cooled Dewoitine D.520, both of which had seen brief service during the Battle of France. There were also the Potez 63 and the NAA-64. I was not qualified to fly the twin-engined Potez, but I did go up a number of times in the North American NAA-64, a two-seat trainer ordered by the French government from the United States before the war.

But the jewel in the crown, perhaps, was my brief hop in an RAF Spitfire. I cannot recall the exact variant, but I believe it was said at the time that it was an example captured intact and shipped back from North Africa. My immediate impression was that the cockpit was a trifle too roomy to let the pilot feel at one with the machine, although that may simply have been my unfamiliarity with it. But otherwise its performance, particularly its ability to turn, was impressive.

At the end of June 1943 I completed my training at Nancy and fondly imagined that, together with my fellow course members, I would now be posted to a front-line fighter unit. But Hauptmann Sommer informed me that I had been selected to serve as an auxiliary fighter instructor, and that I would therefore have to remain at Nancy for a few months longer. This news prompted mixed feelings. On the one hand, I could not suppress a certain measure of pride at this tacit acknowledgement of my flying abilities. But, on the other, I would gladly have foregone this accolade if it meant instead being transferred to the front to begin real operational flying. In hindsight, the order to remain at Nancy very probably increased my life expectancy to a considerable extent.

Within a month, despite my total lack of operational experience, my position as an instructor with JG 107 was made quasi-official and I was given charge of a group of about ten trainees. This allowed me ample opportunity to fly, which I used to the full. The regulations at that time specified that an instructor was permitted to fly no more than four hours a day. I interpreted this rule rather loosely to mean four hours per day *on average*. Thus, after any period of 'QBI' – 'weather unfit for flying', which restricted us to the classroom – I would make up my supposed flying hours by putting in more time in the air during the days that followed. This worked well for a while, but then got me into serious trouble.

One Monday, after a prolonged spell of rain, I clocked up ten training flights, each lasting a full hour. The next day it was eight, and on the Wednesday six. This made a total of twenty-four flying hours over the three days, whereas officially only twelve were allowed. The entire three days had been spent on the Arado Ar 66, a placid little biplane with a landing speed of some 70km/h. But on the Thursday I was scheduled to introduce my charges to the Ar 96, a more powerful and altogether far less forgiving machine, whose landing speed was nearly twice as fast.

While coming in to land after the first of that day's training flights, my mind was fully occupied by the points I needed to get across to the pupils at debriefing. Out of sheer habit I automatically brought the machine down as if still at the controls of an Ar 66. The inevitable result was that my 'crate' ran out of lift while still five metres off the ground. It fell to earth with an almighty wallop, bounced a couple of times, and ended up standing on its nose; a classic 'Fliegerdenkmal', or 'airman's monument', as it was known in the Luftwaffe – and all in plain view of the Geschwaderkommodore.

Horrified, I could scarcely take in at first what had happened. But there was nothing for it; the blame was mine and mine alone. I tried to put as brave a face on things as possible as I clambered carefully out of the cockpit – only to slip and end up on my backside on the ground. The first person to arrive on the scene was the Schirrmeister, the flight sergeant in charge of the workshops, who came pedalling up like fury on his bicycle.

It obviously hadn't registered with him that there was nobody else about. "The arsehole who did this deserves a bloody good smack in the gob, Herr Leutnant," he raged. But when I pointed out that the orifice in question was the one standing in front of him, he calmed down considerably. I may have escaped a smack in the gob, but the official consequences of my accident were not so easily avoided. Charged under Para. 92 of the disciplinary code for damaging Luftwaffe property and failing to observe regulations, I was confined to my quarters for three days and had one-third of my flying pay docked for a period of three months.

Fortunately, I was able to redeem myself somewhat a few weeks later with a nifty, if involuntary piece of flying. I had been detailed to act as wingman to one of the other instructors, a Leutnant with a lot of operational experience under his belt, as that day's readiness Rotte. Our orders were to stand by, prepared to take off in the unit's two Me 109Gs if the alarm was raised – which is precisely what happened when a high-flying British Mosquito reconnaissance aircraft was reported to be in the area.

As it was an emergency scramble we taxied directly from dispersal straight out across the field, with me keeping station some fifty metres to the side of, and slightly behind my number one. After the recent long spell of hot weather the surface of the field was almost bare of grass and bone dry. Red flares were going up to warn all other aircraft to keep their distance. But, unknown to us, one of the trainees flying solo in an Ar 66 had failed to notice all the excitement and was coming in to land diagonally across our path.

By this time we were accelerating rapidly. The tail of my machine was already off the ground. I wasn't tail-dragging because I wanted as much forward visibility as possible over the engine cowling. Not that it did me much good, as I was enveloped in the thick cloud of dust being thrown up by my leader. But suddenly, at the very last moment, I caught a glimpse of a shadowy shape bearing down on me from the right. Instinctively I yanked the stick back into my stomach, at the same time grabbing for the undercarriage retraction lever.

Luckily for me, the Gustav had just enough speed to leave the ground – I must have cleared the Arado by a matter of centimetres at most – but my machine was labouring along left wing low and I hadn't a hope of climbing away. I continued across the field in this attitude until I felt the speed begin to build up. Only then could I bring the aircraft back on to the straight and level and start slowly to gain altitude. In the event, it was all to no avail. When we finally got up to 10,000 metres, the reported height of the Mosquito, there wasn't a thing to be seen.

One day in August Hauptmann Sommer dropped another bombshell. I was to train a group of twenty Bulgarian pilots to fly the Dewoitine D.520. I have to admit that this French fighter was the only aircraft that I ever actively disliked. It had none of the good-natured qualities of the Messerschmitt and was an altogether malicious beast. Take your eye off the airspeed indicator for a single second, dare to drop a fraction below minimum speed and – without the slightest warning – the Dewoitine would immediately stall, tip over on to its left wing and whip into a spin.

Admittedly, recovery was not all that difficult, but it required a good 1,000 metres to get it back on to an even keel. It also had a mind of its own on the ground, and taxiing was an art in itself. The mainwheel airbrakes were controlled by two separate pushbuttons and a pilot's inexperience could be judged by the amount of drunken weaving about he did as he taxied to and from dispersal.

The Bulgarians proved themselves to be extremely competent flyers, however – although their individualistic behaviour, not to say downright indiscipline in the air left a lot to be desired. After a couple of weeks I had got to the stage where I considered each of them fully capable of ferrying a Dewoitine back to Bulgaria. The flight was to be led by their Luftwaffe liaison officer, Hauptmann Hermann Hollweg, and I was ordered to accompany them as a sort of glorified 'dogsbody-cum-refuse collector', tagging along to gather up any stragglers who fell by the wayside and escort them to their destination in the wake of the main flock. After taking delivery of twenty-two fresh Dewoitines from the Toulouse factory, we were ready for the off. For me the flight down to Bulgaria promised to be a very welcome break, not to say a minor adventure. But it was not exactly a pleasure trip the whole way.

In fact, we hit the first snag even before leaving the ground at Nancy. Two of the machines simply refused to start. I had previously decided that I would always be the last to take off in order to be able to help out in case of just such an emergency. This turned out to be absolutely the right thing to do, both now and further down the line. Despite my aversion to the Dewoitine, I had amassed quite a bit of experience on the type and we soon had the engines running. The three of us then took off to chase after the others.

Our final destination was the airfield at Karlovo, some 150 kilometres to the southeast of the Bulgarian capital, Sofia. The flight was to be made in three stages, with overnight stops at Wiener Neustadt and Belgrade on the way. Shortly after leaving Nancy my two free-spirited Bulgarians began to wander about all over the sky. We had no radio contact with each other, and so I had no means of stopping them swooping down to poke their noses into the occasional Black Forest valley or whatever else happened to catch their interest. One moment they would be in reasonably close contact with me; the next they were so far away that I would be afraid of losing sight of them altogether.

But as we crossed the River Inn and approached the Alps, the weather began to close in threateningly. And – lo and behold – suddenly there they both were, anxiously tucked in behind me like a couple of chicks behind a mother hen. We sneaked in to Wiener Neustadt just ahead of the bad weather front and en-joyed a convivial evening in the mess with the main party, who had arrived not long before us.

Next morning's planned take-off was a repeat performance of the Nancy episode – except this time *three* of the Dewoitines refused to start. Try as we might, we couldn't get all three run-ning in unison. One engine would finally be coaxed into life, only to expire as soon as we turned our backs on it to attend to the other two. This happened time and again. It was a full hour and a half before we were eventually able to get off the ground. It was a Sunday, the previous night's storm had abated and the weather was perfect. It had all the makings of a very pleasant flight. But, in fact, all it did was to persuade the three clowns I had with me today to indulge in even more idiotic antics.

The route we had been given didn't help much either. Soon after crossing into Hungarian airspace we found ourselves flying over the sun-dappled surface of Lake Balaton. It seemed as if every weekend sailor from Budapest and beyond was taking advantage of the glorious weather. The lake was dotted with yachts of every shape and size. It was all too much for my over-excitable companions. One after the other they peeled away from me in elegant diving turns. Moments later they were low over the glittering waters of the lake weaving in and out between the yachts.

It made a pretty picture from my vantage point on high. But it also made my hair stand on end, for I soon realized that they were not simply flying around between the yachts – they were actually using them as targets to carry out practice low-level attacks! The terrified boat owners stood absolutely no chance of getting out of the way, of course, and I was fervently praying that the inevitable wouldn't happen... when the inevitable happened. One of the yachts was capsized by the slipstream from a D.520 roaring past too close alongside it.

This evidently shocked some sense into my three musketeers. They climbed back up to me and sheepishly resumed what might loosely be termed formation, at least until we had the low range of hills around Fünfkirchen (Pécs) safely behind us. Not long afterwards we crossed the Danube at Mohács and from there the northern Yugoslav plain stretched ahead of us all the way down to Belgrade. Having recovered their high spirits, my companions now amused themselves by beating up the small villages and isolated farmsteads that lay along our route.

We landed at Belgrade/Semlin around noon and the first thing I did was to offer up a prayer of thanks that nothing more serious had occurred and that no complaint regarding the incident on Lake Balaton had come in. Then I gave vent to my feelings in a torrent of words and gestures; the latter no doubt being the more intelligible to the three bemused Bulgarians. I also had to make my report to Hauptmann Hollweg, who conveyed the gist of my remarks to the trio in their own language. At least they had the grace to look contrite.

The final leg to Karlovo – with me again bringing up the rear having first had to cajole two more recalcitrant Hispano-Suiza engines into reluctant life – was a model of mid-European discipline. This was perhaps not all that surprising, given that our route took us along the Morava River to Nis and thence through the Pirot Pass, which was Yugoslav partisan-held territory for most of the way.

When we arrived at Karlovo the Dewoitines of the main group were already drawn up in a long immaculate line as if on parade. This did not deter my two wingmen from expressing their joy at a safe return home by making a low-level pass across the field, waggling their wings and almost flattening the grass in their wake.

Then it was time to make ourselves presentable and report to the CO of the field's resident Bulgarian fighter wing. This worthy welcomed Hollweg and me in true Slav fashion with a passionate embrace and kisses on both cheeks. We were conducted to our quarters in the nearby resort town, where a party in our honour had been arranged for the evening. This turned into just about the most riotous gathering I have ever attended in my entire life. We had naturally assumed that proceedings would kick off in the accepted fashion with a hearty meal. But we were sadly mistaken.

The revellers got down to hard drinking straight away, with only the odd morsel of food passing our lips between sessions devoted to emptying every bottle that was placed in front of us. The whole crowd soon became extremely loud and extremely cheerful. But these lads could certainly hold their alcohol. It must have been very close to midnight before the party reached its frenetic climax. And it wasn't just the champagne corks that were popping; pistols and all kinds of other weapons were being emptied into the ceiling and a fine rain of plaster was drizzling down, coating us all in a thin layer of white dust. In the midst of all this tumult and mayhem, loud toasts and bucolic vows of eternal friendship filled the large room. It was a scene of complete chaos.

Next morning – nearer midday, to be more precise – pale, zombie-like figures could be seen shambling about, each in their own alcoholic daze. One of these apparitions had been detailed to fly me to Sofia, where Hauptmann Hollweg and I had been invited to visit Commander Alexandrov and his sister, who was a stage actress currently appearing at the capital's main theatre. I wasn't in the most sober of conditions myself, but when I walked out to the Bücker Bü 131 and saw the state of my new bosom friend, Stefan Marinopolski, who was unsteadily holding on to the machine's wing for dear life, I had a quick change of heart.

"If I'm for the chop," I decided, "I'll be the one wielding the axe." I motioned that I would pilot the aircraft. Stefan peered at me through swollen, half-closed eyes and seemed about to argue the point. But then he gave in and accepted the situation. So the pair of us strapped ourselves in and managed to reach the Bulgarian capital without mishap. There Hollweg and I spent a very pleasant and civilized evening in the charming company of the Alexandrovs. The following morning we boarded a Junkers Ju 52 transport for the return flight, via Vienna, to Nancy.

During the remaining weeks of that September 1943 I was kept fully occupied teaching a new group of trainees the skills needed for combat flying. It was a rewarding task, but my proficiency at it was a double-edged sword. For their part, personnel and postings were no doubt congratulating themselves on having fitted a round peg neatly into a round hole. From my point of view, however, I was all too conscious of the fact that I had not yet fired a shot in anger and was still as far away from an operational unit as ever.

But with the job in hand requiring my complete and undivided attention, there was little time to dwell on such matters. While fully aware that the tide of war was turning, my fellow instructors and I lived each day as it came. The news that trickled through to us of the terrible sufferings being endured both by the civilian populations of Germany's bombed cities and by our comrades on the fighting fronts affected us deeply. But, we reasoned, it could only be a matter of time before our turn came.

What didn't enter our heads was that we could lose the war. We were so thoroughly steeped in the official line of thinking that such a possibility simply didn't occur to us – although our indoctrination did not preclude the occasional wry smile at some of the wilder flights of propaganda fancy emanating from our lords and masters. For us one thing was certain: the war had to be won. Defeat and everything that would come after it was out of the question.

Before leaving the subject of my time at Nancy, however, there is one episode which, although it has little to do with my flying activities, perhaps deserves mention. It is etched for all time in my memory as 'Annelies's Birthday'. Among the staff in our admin offices were a number of so-called 'Stabshelferinnen'. These were civilian German female auxiliaries who, as a kind of national service, had been drafted in to work as typists, secretaries and the like for the armed forces. As a rule they were young unmarried girls.

Those employed at Nancy did not live on the base, but were billeted in a large requisitioned school outside of town on the edge of the plateau about one kilometre away. The school and its extensive grounds were strictly off limits to all male personnel, of course. I had been seeing quite a lot of one of the girls – the aforementioned Annelies – and, knowing that her birthday

84

was coming up, I had booked us a table at one of Nancy's top restaurants for dinner that evening. I had also arranged my training schedule so that we could spend the afternoon together as well. It was a fine summer Sunday and I suggested several places that we could visit or things that we could do, but Annelies didn't appear all that keen on any of my ideas. She clearly had something else in mind, but seemed unwilling, or unable, to tell me what it was.

"Come on, Annelies," I prompted, "if you've got some other suggestion, spit it out." "Look, I tell you what," she said with a slight shrug, "why don't I bake us a nice cake, make a pot of coffee, and then we can have a picnic in the field behind the school. There'll be hardly anyone else around. A lot of the girls are away on holiday and the others will be working, so nobody will see us." I was dumbstruck at first, and said we couldn't possibly risk it. But, to be honest, the more I thought about it, the more appealing it became. After all, if Adam could give in to temptation, who was I to hold out. And so, immediately after lunch in the officers' mess, I jumped on my bike and pedalled up to the plateau. (That was my first punishable offence of the day, for it was strictly against standing orders to take a service bicycle off the station. And with a yellow '5' painted on its frame – yellow for 3. Staffel – my two-wheeled steed was all too clearly an item of service equipment.)

As it was a Sunday and all the shops were shut, I had been unable to buy any flowers. But I had everything else we needed for the picnic. For her part, Annelies had the coffee and cake all ready and waiting. We carried the things out into the large secluded meadow, surrounded by trees, that stretched away to the rear of the school. Choosing a nice cosy corner, we trampled a circle some three metres wide in the lush waist-high grass, spread the cloth, laid out the crockery and began the birthday party. I was able to devote my full attention to Annelies, for we could not be overlooked and the spot we had selected was perfectly hidden... or so we thought.

After we had finished our picnic, matters started to take their natural course – as matters do – and the realities of the outside world faded into oblivion. In my subconscious I was dimly aware of the sounds of various aircraft taking off and landing on the airfield below. I registered the deep-throated roar of a Me 109's engine being run up, and then the tinnier note of our Fieseler Storch taking off. With its remarkably low speed of just fifty-five kilometres an hour, the Storch was the favourite mount of our Gruppenkommandeur, who would regularly use it to go boar hunting.

We normally welcomed these expeditions of his, for he rarely returned empty-handed and our cook could always be counted upon to conjure up the most succulent game roasts for the mess table. But on this occasion the noise of the Storch taking to the air should have set the alarm bells jangling in my head. By this time, however, Annelies and I had got to the stage where four of my five senses were no longer functioning properly. Then suddenly – but far too late – I heard a distinctive rustling sound in the air. It was rapidly getting louder and coming closer. We glanced up and to our horror saw the Fieseler Storch, its engine switched off, glide into view just above the tops of the trees.

Scrambling quickly apart, Annelies and I both stared upwards... straight into the eyes of the Gruppenkommandeur, who was looking down at us through the side window of the steeply banking Storch. With a tiny squeal Annelies, wearing nothing but a signet ring, immediately threw herself onto her stomach – a natural enough reaction under the circumstances, I suppose, but one which did little to retrieve the situation.

As for myself, programmed as I was by years of military training, my first instinct in the presence of a superior officer was to salute! But how? I was also lying in the grass without a stitch on. Had I been wearing my cap, I might have got away with a normal military salute – fingers touching the peak: 'like this', as we used to call it. Without headgear one was supposed to salute 'like that', which meant performing the 'Heil Hitler' greeting but without actually saying the words. However, as one part of my anatomy was still giving a very fair imitation of the 'Heil Hitler', I felt that raising my right arm as well might perhaps be over-doing things.

While these ridiculous thoughts were racing through my head, the Storch had disappeared – and so too had our party mood. Furious that her birthday had been ruined, Annelies had got to her knees. Every curve quivering with rage, she hurled some very un-ladylike epithets after the departed Storch. "You just wait and see," she turned to me still boiling with anger, "I bet he shops you to the Kommodore." "Nonsense," I replied, "he's got enough rank to haul me over the coals himself. He doesn't need any extra help." Dejectedly we began to gather our things together. The birthday party was well and truly over.

During dinner in the mess that evening – the restaurant booking had been cancelled by mutual consent – the Geschwader-adjutant unexpectedly appeared at my table with an evil grin on his face: "Right then, Fischer, report to the Kommodore's office tomorrow at 13.30 hours. I'm sure you already know why." So Annalies had been right after all. That cowardly swine must really have wanted my hide nailed to the wall if he was prepared to take the matter to the Kommodore. But there was nothing I could do about it, no excuses I could make; the 'bare facts' spoke for themselves.

My only recourse was to make myself as smart and present-able as possible, report to the Kommodore as ordered, and take whatever 'Old Frau Mayer' had in store for me. (Just how the Geschwaderkommodore had acquired this nickname nobody knew. He was admittedly somewhat older – around the forty

An aerial view of wartime Nancy looking from the railway station towards the infamous plateau, scene of 'Annelies's birthday', in the background.

mark, I would guess – but he was wiry, an accomplished flyer, and by no stretch of the imagination an 'old woman'.)

And so, on the Monday morning, one of the pupils helped me get my service dress uniform into as near immaculate a condition as possible. Tunic and breeches were brushed and ironed, steel helmet dusted off, leather belt and boots polished until they gleamed. Shortly before the appointed 13.30 hours I marched off to the Kommodore's office. Suited and booted, helmeted and gloved, pistol holster pertly positioned against my right buttock, I looked like something that had just stepped straight out of a Luftwaffe recruitment poster.

Trainees I passed on the way saluted me with knowing grins. So the story had got around already. As I walked through the main office it was even worse. "Did you at least enjoy it, Herr Leutnant?" the giggling typists called after me. Cheeky young baggages! Then I was outside his office door, which was guarded by a distinguished, blue-blooded lady of more mature years.

"Would you please be so kind as to report my presence, madam", I requested politely. "At once, Herr Fischer", she responded with a decidedly supercilious smile. She opened the door, "Leutnant Fischer reporting as ordered, Herr Oberstleutnant." "Show him in!!!" a loud voice roared. I already had visions of another three days confined to quarters – and the ink was hardly dry on the charge sheet for the last three, awarded for cracking up that Ar 96 on landing. "Bags of swank", I said to myself as I fairly burst into the Kommodore's office, slamming my heels together so hard that the windows almost rattled in their frames.

I stared fixedly from beneath the rim of my steel helmet, my eyes boring directly into his, stiffened to attention – chin out, stomach in, middle fingers in line with the seams of my breeches, elbows bent slightly forward and my feet almost at right angles – saluted, and shouted aloud in ringing tones, "Leutnant Fischer respectfully begs to report!!" My voice didn't have the same formidable volume as his invitation of a moment ago for me to enter, but... hang on a minute... what's this: he's sitting behind his desk looking perfectly relaxed and is regarding me in a not altogether unkindly fashion.

He rose from his chair and slowly walked around me, inspecting my uniform closely as if afraid that a button might be undone and that I could be in danger of catching a cold. Obviously reassured that all was well and that there was little likelihood of my having to report sick, he returned to his seat.

"Well, my son (my son?!), let me give you a piece of good advice: should you ever get the urge to do 'it' again – (at twenty-one, I thought, you've always got the urge) – I suggest that you sneak into the bushes with your lady friend and do not spread yourselves out in the middle of an open meadow, especially not one right next to an airfield. That way you won't be mistaken for a pair of wild boars, you blockheads! And now get out of here!"

I have never left a superior's office so rapidly in all my life. Now it was my turn to smile as I dashed past the dragon on the door. It felt as if a huge weight had been lifted off my shoulders as I almost ran through the main office, giving the thumbs up to the applauding typists. A few days later I heard that after I had scuttled out of his office Old Frau Mayer had laughed so much that the tears ran down his cheeks.

By the end of September 1943 I had served a full three months as an instructor with JG 107. I was still fervently hoping to be relieved of these training duties and get a posting to an operational unit. But it seemed the authorities were unwilling to dispense with my services just yet, for Hauptmann Sommer informed me that on 1 October I was to be sent to Guyancourt near Versailles to begin yet *another* three-month course that would see me emerge at the end of the year as a fully-qualified fighter instructor.

Unintentionally, I'm sure, he then proceeded to rub salt into my wounds by telling me that his own stint with JG 107 was coming to a close and that he was returning to a front-line unit. He had been appointed Staffelkapitän of 3./JG 2 Richthofen in western France, currently one of the Luftwaffe's hottest operational areas. Sentenced to embark on a course that was intended to transform me into a bona fide instructor, my own flying future appeared to be heading in completely the opposite direction. Nevertheless, I asked Hauptmann Sommer – implored might not be too strong a word – to put in an official request for me to join his Staffel when I had completed my three months at Guyancourt, and this he faithfully promised to do.

My new unit was known as the Jagdlehrerüberprüfungs-gruppe – literally the 'Fighter Instructors' Inspection Group'. Activated a year earlier at Orléans-Bricy, it had been transferred to Guyancourt only a month prior to my arrival. Commanded by Hauptmann Ferdinand Vögl, its purpose was to meet the growing demand for qualified instructors from the Luftwaffe's many fighter training schools. The Gruppe consisted of just two Staffeln: the main Ausbildungsstaffel (training Staffel) under Oberleutnant Magnus Brunkhorst, and the smaller Einsatzstaffel (operational Staffel) commanded by Oberleutnant Alfons Raich. In addition to its advanced training duties, the Einsatzstaffel was also required to keep a Schwarm at readiness as part of the aerial defences of the Greater Paris area.

The three months I was to spend at Guyancourt added significantly both to the number of flying hours piling up in my logbook and to my theoretical knowledge of air combat. But otherwise, apart from a slightly greater emphasis on the instructor's duties in the classroom, they added little new to what I had already been doing at Nancy. The little new did, however, include my transition to the Focke-Wulf Fw 190A fighter. I was immediately won over by the radial-engined Focke-Wulf, finding it far more advanced and robustly constructed than the Me 109, which, to be frank, was beginning to show its age.

Whereas, for example, the wings of the Messerschmitt were attached to the machine's fuselage by a set of bolts no thicker than a man's thumb, which meant that they could shear off in dives of more than 800 km/h, the Focke-Wulf's fuselage was mounted squarely on a solid wing centre-section carry-through that enabled it to reach speeds of over 950 km/h (the highest figure shown on the clock) when diving. The machine built up speed remarkably rapidly in the dive, but was nonetheless easily controllable – although recovery did require a fair amount of physical strength on the part of the pilot when pulling back on the stick.

The 1,800hp BMW 801 air-cooled two-row radial engine did admittedly run a little less sweetly than the Me 109's liquid-cooled Daimler-Benz. It had a certain rough undertone that took some getting used to. But the Focke-Wulf's wide-tracked undercarriage – the mainwheel legs were attached well out along the wing and retracted inwards – meant that take-offs and landings posed few problems. A slight tendency to swing to the left could be easily held on the rudder. The bulky engine cowling, however, did severely limit forward visibility when on the ground. This was something of a liability as the standard procedure at take-off was to drag the tail. If the self-centring tailwheel lost contact with the ground too quickly, the high-speed wing profile was unable to lift the machine into the air and it had to be literally heaved off the ground bodily.

The Focke-Wulf had the edge over the Messerschmitt in many other ways too. For example, its systems were all electric. While the Me 109's engine had to be cranked by hand to get it going, the Fw 190's BMW was served by an inertia starter energized either by an external electrical supply or by the fighter's own battery. Flaps and trim also had to be operated by hand in the Messerschmitt. They were infinitely adjustable by electric switch and button in the Focke-Wulf.

The Fw 190 was better in the turn, marginally faster up to a height of 8,000 metres, and the all-round view from its fully glazed canopy was excellent. All in all, it was a great improvement on the Me 109, except for one thing: engine performance at altitudes above 8,000 metres. Here the Messerschmitt was unquestionably dominant. But this was not too important as ninety-five percent of all fighter combats took place below that height and, as a rule, most enemy bombers rarely flew above 6,500 metres at this stage of the war. In any case, the Focke-Wulf's dive and climb capabilities were so superior that its pilot could usually dictate at which height any engagement was to be fought.

The humdrum routine of the Guyancourt training programme was occasionally enlivened by our being called upon to participate in manoeuvres with the ground forces. This gave us the perfect excuse to thunder about all over the place, indulge in low-level beat-ups and generally fool around with a complete disregard for aerial safety and discipline. Looking back on our antics today, when a pilot's prowess is rated in terms of the safe and responsible handling of his machine at all times and in all situations, I can only shake my head in disbelief at what we got up to – and got away *with* – back in those less regulated days. The one abiding memory of my time at Guyancourt concerns not the Fw 190, however, but the much more humble Bü 131 Jungmann biplane.

I had been detailed to fly another member of the Gruppe across to Orly; for what particular reason I can no longer recall. Back then Orly was just a small and fairly unimportant airfield to the south of Paris. After landing we strolled across to the officers' mess where, although it was well past lunchtime, a couple of attractive young French girls still busy in the kitchen rustled us up something to eat.

When we had finished our meal – we were alone in the dining room – we put a popular hit record of the day on the mess gramophone and invited our two companions to dance. But our afternoon idyll was soon rudely interrupted by the station commander, who ordered me to fly back to Guyancourt forthwith. I was about halfway back to base, bumbling comfortably along some 400 metres above the French countryside, but still feeling a bit irritated and wondering what I could do to lift my spirits, when ahead of me I spotted some sort of racetrack, presumably used at one time by either cars or motorcycles.

As I got closer I could see that it was laid out in a typical oval shape with banked curves and it suddenly occurred to me that my Bücker's cruising speed of just over 150 km/h was probably not very much faster than that of the vehicles which had once raced on the track. I carefully descended into the circuit and, sure enough, found that I could follow the banking quite easily. This prompted me to do a couple of laps, my wheels never more than two metres above the concrete surface of the track. After scattering out of the way, some civilian workmen watched my impromptu performance open-mouthed. Luckily, they obviously didn't bother to make a note of my machine's markings, for I completed my trip back to Guyancourt in a much better frame of mind and was never questioned about the incident.

But such joyriding was becoming increasingly hazardous as the war situation worsened and allied bombers and fighter-bombers began to appear in the skies of northern and central France in ever-larger numbers. It was perhaps as a result of this growing threat that the Jagdlehrerüberprüfungsgruppe received orders in late December to vacate Guyancourt for the relative safety of southern France. The Gruppe divided its strength between Aix-en-Provence and Orange-Caritat. And it was at Aix that we celebrated the end of our course with Christmas dinner in the station mess.

A few days later I returned to JG 107 at Nancy. Although now an officially qualified fighter-instructor, I was still hoping against hope that Hauptmann Sommer's promised intervention would result in an operational posting to 3./JG 2. But whatever requests he may have made on my behalf had apparently fallen on deaf ears, for I was immediately sent away on yet another course – would the damn things never end? – and one, moreover, that saw me heading off in a completely unexpected direction; not just geographically, but in terms of my flying career too.

My destination lay in the very heart of Germany: at Altenburg, south of Leipzig, in the province of Thuringia. This was the home of Hauptmann Albert Falderbaum's I./JG 110. Like most of the 'new' training Jagdgeschwadern at that time, JG 110 had been created simply by redesignating an existing school unit. In JG 110's case this had been Blindflugschule 10, or Blind-Flying School 10. As its name suggests, BFS 10 had been involved in the training of night-fighter pilots – but a very specific kind of night-fighter pilot. Set up at Altenburg in May 1943, BFS 10's job was to train pilots in the Wilde Sau ('Wild Boar') method of night fighting.

Unlike the Luftwaffe's standard night-fighter units, whose twin-engined machines were radar-equipped and radar-controlled, the Wilde Sau system – the brainchild of ex-bomber pilot Major Hajo Herrmann – operated single-seat fighters and relied on visual sighting to locate the enemy's night bombers. Initially intended merely to supplement the Luftwaffe's established night-fighter organization, Wilde Sau operations had proved surprisingly effective during the late summer/early autumn of 1943 and three new Jagdgeschwadern had already been activated as dedicated Wilde Sau units. Presumably it was to one of these three that I would now be going after completing my two months' training at Altenburg.

The course commenced at the beginning of January 1944. My only previous night flying experience had been those few tentative circuits at Bad Wörishofen back in late 1942. Since then I had been trained solely as a day-fighter pilot. But despite a certain sense of disappointment at the turn events had taken, I must admit that the eight weeks spent at Altenburg broadened my flying experience enormously. At first, going up at night, sometimes in total darkness, seemed quite a risky business to me. But after getting used to the additional instruments in the aircraft, and learning the radio procedures that linked the pilot in the air to ground control, night flying became more of a routine. It never lost its fascination altogether, however, and cruising about on my own in the night sky always filled me with a sense of adventure.

I./JG 110 had a number of two-seat trainer biplanes on

strength. These were used to initiate the trainees into the art of blind flying. The pupil's seat – usually at the front in the Arado Ar 66, but at the back in the Gotha Go 145 – could be covered by a hood that excluded all daylight. Flying in complete darkness, the trainee had to rely entirely on his instruments to follow the instructor's orders over the R/T; just as later he would have to follow the commands received from his ground controller.

In between our blind-flying training flights, we were given classroom tuition on the theory and practice of Wilde Sau operations. Basically, it was a very simple concept. Ground control would vector the high flying pilot towards the area under attack, usually a large conurbation, where the RAF bombers below him would be silhouetted against the massed searchlights of the defences, the fires raging on the ground and the enemy's own marker flares. Even if the ground was obscured by solid cloud, control could order searchlight batteries to illuminate the base of the clouds so that, again, the attacking bombers would be clearly visible in silhouette 'crawling across the sky like bugs on a pane of frosted glass'. Once visual contact had been established, the Wilde Sau pilot was free to formulate his own plan of attack.

After attaining the necessary level of proficiency in night flying, we were sent up solo. The machine generally used during this stage of our training was the Me 109. This was chosen because an experienced pilot, as those of us on the course all were, could judge the speed of an Me remarkably accurately purely from the amount of pressure that needed to be applied to the stick and by the noise of the slipstream. This meant that he did not constantly have to look down at his airspeed indicator.

The most difficult part of a Wilde Sau sortie, as indeed of any flight, was the landing. But we were helped down by a rudimentary beam approach system that guided the pilot towards the runway. A succession of cross beams at regular intervals gave him his height and distance from the end of the runway, and if he started to wander off course the steady tone in his headphones would give way to a series of either dots or dashes. Shortly before touchdown the runway lights would be switched on briefly to allow him to make any necessary final corrections.

It was a lot to assimilate, but at the end of our eight weeks at Altenburg we were duly awarded our CIII blind-flying certificates. By this time, however – it was now the end of February 1944 – Wilde Sau operations were no longer achieving quite the same level of success as they had enjoyed when first introduced. The wintry weather conditions were certainly a contributory factor in their decline. But it was the growing intensity of the American daylight bombing offensive that called the whole programme into question and ultimately led to its demise. Single-seat night-fighter operations would be largely abandoned by the early summer of 1944, with the three Jagdgeschwadern that constituted the Wilde Sau force being remustered as all-weather fighter units. Perhaps as a consequence of this uncertainty, our course was not sent en bloc to the Wilde Sau organization.

I, for one, was both surprised and overjoyed to discover that my long-cherished ambition had at last been realized... a posting to a day-fighter unit. And not just any day-fighter unit either, but to JG 2 Richthofen, the very Geschwader I had wanted. Coincidence? Or had Hauptmann Sommer come up trumps after all?

CHAPTER 6

POSTED TO
THE FRONT

It had been a long, and at times incomprehensible road. Trained to be a fighter pilot, I had been made a temporary instructor. Qualifying as an instructor, I had been sent to a night-fighter school. Gaining my blind-flying certificate, I had been posted to a day-fighter Geschwader. But now that road was finally behind me. And the journey, I felt, had been well worthwhile.

I had been ordered to report to JG 2's Ergänzungs unit, which was currently based some 260 kilometres to the east of Altenburg at Liegnitz in Silesia. In the Luftwaffe scheme of things, every front-line Jagdgeschwader had initially had its own Ergänzungsstaffel, literally 'replenishment squadron'. This had served as a kind of 'in-house OTU', where pilots fresh from training schools would be given a final check over by the Geschwader's own pilots before being let loose on actual operations. Most of these early Staffeln had subsequently been increased to Gruppe strength, before a major reorganization in 1942 led to their all being amalgamated into three specialized and enlarged Ergänzungsjagdgruppen: South, East and West.

Each individual Staffel still retained its connections to, and continued to supply replacement pilots for, its own parent Jagdgeschwader, however. And it was to JG 2's Staffel, currently operating as 1./EJGr West, that I was now heading. The knowledge that I was about to join the Luftwaffe's premier Jagdgeschwader helped soften the expected blow of yet more training. For upon arrival at an Ergänzungs unit, every new pilot usually underwent a four-week 'final polish'. This was intended to acquaint him with the tactics and conditions relevant to the particular combat zone in which he would be operating.

But I was spared this last rung on the training ladder due to the length of time I had already served as a fighter instructor preparing other pilots for front-line service. I therefore remained at Liegnitz only long enough to pick up my travel warrants from the admin office. My next destination, I discovered, was to be JG 2's Geschwaderstab (wing HQ) based at Marines to the northwest of Paris.

The air war over northwest Europe was escalating alarmingly. It was at this time, on 2 March 1944, that JG 2 lost its Kommodore of eight months' standing when Oberstleutnant Egon Mayer, an ace with 102 victories to his credit – twenty-five of them four-engined bombers – was killed in action against American P-47 Thunderbolt fighters near Montmédy close to the Franco-Belgian border. I did not fully appreciate the pressure the Geschwader was under during this period, for hardly had I arrived at Marines before I was on my way again, being despatched almost immediately to the Wing's I. Gruppe, which had been deployed down to Aix-en-Provence in southern France at the beginning of the year. Aix was already familiar to me from the few days I had spent there with the Jagdlehrerüberprüfungsgruppe at the end of 1943. My second visit was to be equally brief.

In the temporary absence of the Gruppenkommandeur,

Major Erich Hohagen, I was welcomed by the senior MO, Oberstabsarzt Klappich. A larger than life character, whose solid build belied his inevitable nickname of 'Klapprich', or 'Rickety', the doctor went out of his way to put me at my ease. Somewhat unusually for a man of his calling, he even explained to me in great detail exactly how to shoot down a Spitfire! Only two of the Gruppe's four component Staffeln were currently in residence at Aix. But the anti-malaria jab that I was given clearly indicated that I was destined for one of the other two: either 3. or 4./JG 2, both of which were then operating over central Italy.

It took me three days by rail to make the journey from Aix to Viterbo, some forty-five kilometres to the north of Rome. There a Kübelwagen and driver were waiting to chauffeur me through a scenic landscape steeped in history to Canino, where our two Staffeln were based. The airfield was situated a few kilometres outside the village on an open plain at the foot of Monte Canino, whose distinctive shape, so my knowledgeable driver informed me, provided a very useful landmark in bad weather.

On arrival at Canino I was shocked to hear that my erstwhile instructor, Hauptmann Sommer, had been killed in action just a few days earlier. In fact, he had been shot down on 14 March – while attacking a formation of enemy medium bombers, it was believed – although nobody seemed sure of the exact circumstances. I will always remember him as a very outgoing and sociable type. At Nancy he would often invite the course leader, Oberleutnant Lesch, and myself to his room where he would proudly serve us a so-called 'Kalter Arsch', or 'cold arse', which he had prepared himself. This dish consisted of nothing more than layers of biscuits soaked in brandy with chilled liquid chocolate in between, but it was typical of the man to go to such lengths to entertain his guests.

100

A more pleasant surprise was to find those two old comrades from my days with the air warfare school at Fürstenfeldbruck, Peter Ullmann and Otto Wania, both of whom were serving with 4./JG 2, the Staffel to which I had been assigned. And when I reported to the Staffelkapitän, I discovered that he was no stranger to me either. Hauptmann Georg Schröder had been treated as a special case by JG 107 at Nancy, being given one-on-one tuition by Hauptmann Sommer while I acted as 'training assistant'. He was a fair bit older than the average pupil – a good thirty, I would guess – and had previously been a course leader with FFS A/B 123, the Luftwaffe elementary flying training school based at Agram (today's Zagreb) in Croatia.

I thought his volunteering for fighter training and subsequent combat duty was highly commendable, even though I did not find him all that sympathetic as a person at the time – which just goes to show how wrong first impressions can be. After being appointed Gruppenkommandeur of II./JG 2 in May 1944, Hauptmann Schröder was to be shot down and captured during Operation Bodenplatte, the Luftwaffe's costly New Year's Day attack on enemy airfields in northwest Europe on 1 January 1945. We were to meet up again in Munich long after the war when he was a completely different character. Freed from command responsibilities and mellowed by civilian life, he proved to be a very agreeable acquaintance and old comrade, with whom I remained in close touch until his death in 1993.

The unexpected presence of Paul and Otto at Canino, and the renewal of friendships first made at F Bruck, meant that my assimilation into the Staffel was both smooth and easy. But having finally arrived at the sharp end of the fighting, I now quickly discovered for myself that the reports on the progress of the war published in our press were clearly intended for home consumption and bore very little relationship to the realities of the front.

At the time of my posting to Italy there could be no question of our still enjoying air superiority; at least, not in the west. Allied numbers were growing by the day. Technically, too, our machines no longer had the edge. For pilots like ourselves flying the Me 109, the British Spitfire and American Thunderbolt were proving particularly hard nuts to crack. As a consequence our own losses were increasing the whole time. This naturally had an effect on morale. While remaining high, it was no longer based on the conviction of certain victory that had characterized the early years of the war – now it was more a feeling of standing with our backs to the wall and having no alternative. Despite everything, however, we still retained a semblance of our boyish humour, even if it was more often than not of the gallows variety.

For the past eight weeks and more, JG 2's two Italian-based Staffeln had been operating with some success against the Anglo-American beachhead at Anzio. Now they were on the point of being rotated back to the relative peace and quiet of Aix-en-Provence for rest and recuperation. Our Staffel was equipped with the Me 109G-6 and before departure for southern France two refurbished Gustavs had to be collected from the works at Perugia. These machines had been assigned to Peter Ullmann and myself and we were detailed to go and fetch them.

Immediately upon take-off from Perugia I could tell that the trim settings on my machine were completely wrong. So much so, in fact, that the moment I took the pressure off the rudder the aircraft immediately tipped over into a violent dive to the left. I was able to adjust the tailplane incidence to some extent by means of the trim wheel down beside my seat, but had to keep the stick pulled back hard to the right to compensate for the incorrect rudder setting. What I should have done, of course, was to put down at Perugia again and have the problem corrected at once. But I knew that there were no operations on the cards for that day as the flight back to Aix was scheduled for early the next morning and so, with the light already beginning to fade, I decided to continue on to Canino, make the return flight to Aix with the rest of the Staffel, and have the trim sorted out there.

At 09.00hrs the following morning – 6 April 1944 – our eight machines lifted off from Canino for the one-and-a-half-hour hop across the Mediterranean to southern France. Each of the Gustavs was fully armed and carrying the maximum amount of fuel, including a 300-litre ventral drop tank. We pilots had stuffed all our worldly goods into the small luggage space at the back of the cockpit. Among my items were my camera, a 9.5mm cine-camera and my prized photo album.

We had set course northwestwards aiming to cross out over the coast near Grosseto. After about twenty minutes we were at a height of around 1,500 metres just south of Grosseto when I noticed fountains of earth climbing into the air close to a railway bridge. At that very same moment the 'Old Man' shouted an urgent warning over the R/T, "Achtung, Mustangs!" Several hundred metres below us were some two-dozen British P-51 Mustangs with roundels on their fuselages and wings. One group was diving in line astern attacking the bridge, while the rest seemed to be concentrating on the town's railway station.

All thoughts of a peaceful and uneventful ferry flight back to France were forgotten. Our first priority now was to tackle these 'Indianer' – 'Indians' was our codeword for all enemy fighters. Initially, our greater height gave us a brief tactical advantage, which we were able to capitalize on. Jettisoning our belly tanks, we dived down and quickly accounted for six of the enemy machines.

The remaining Indianer promptly scattered and the encounter fragmented into a series of bitter individual dogfights with aircraft twisting and turning no more than 100 metres off the ground. Outnumbered and with the element of surprise gone, we found ourselves hard pressed. Four Gustavs were shot down, but fortunately we suffered no casualties other than the slightly wounded Leutnant Schorsch Schneider, who took a small calibre bullet cleanly through the left wrist as he was bal- ing out.

Having settled myself comfortably into the cockpit, intent on enjoying the glorious weather and the fascinating landscape unfolding beneath my wings, it had come as an enormous shock to me when our routine ferry flight suddenly turned into my first combat mission – and no easy one at that, for we were facing odds of at least three to one against. So abrupt was the turn of events that there was no time for the queasy feeling in the pit of my stomach that I would later come to experience while awaiting the order to scramble against an approaching enemy. One moment I was cruising along without a care in the world, the next I was putting into practice all those skills I had amassed while training. And it immediately became clear that I was going to need every single one of them, not just to distract the Mustangs from their bombing, but to save my own skin.

For as soon as our formation had been split apart, I was sin- gled out by three of the enemy fighters, who came at me head on. I stood the Gustav on its wingtip and pulled a Gerissene Kurve – the manoeuvre described on page 69 – which gained me some breathing space. I was now behind the three Tommys, who had flashed past me in line abreast. But their reactions were lightning-fast and I was soon under pressure again. I em- ployed every trick I knew, juggling flaps and throttle to prevent any of my three opponents from getting on my tail.

But it couldn't last. I lost track of one of the P-51s for a split second. I caught sight of him again a moment later, but it was already too late – he was barrelling in on me from one side. I yanked the Me's nose up in a desperate effort to escape his fire, but felt the machine jolt as it was hit – in the underside of the engine cowling, I thought. The bang was accompanied by my first true 'whiff of powder', but a quick glance at the instrument panel told me that nothing vital had been hit. The Gustav was still answering to the controls and the uneven contest continued.

Once or twice I even managed to jockey into position behind one of my opponents. But it was never long enough to get off a carefully aimed burst of fire and before having to take violent evasive action as another of the trio came boring in at me again. Then I had a stroke of luck. Two of the P-51s got in each other's way and were forced to break off for a few vital seconds. In the meantime I had just succeeded in latching on to the tail of the third. He was right down on the deck and I was all of twenty metres above him. With my excess of speed I was able rapidly to close in on him. At a range of thirty metres I had a perfect close-up view of my adversary. His engine cowling, cockpit and wing root area filled my Revi gunsight. It was impossible to miss.

But it was at that precise moment that Lady Luck decided to transfer her allegiance to the Tommy pilot – or my 'comrade from the other FPO number', as we often referred to our aerial opponents. My guns jammed! Despite my frantic attempts to recharge them, they refused to fire. That earlier hit in the engine cowling must have damaged the so-called 'Waffenautomat', the device mounted below the engine block that governed all the on-board weapons. The few seconds I spent wrestling with my guns had enabled the other two P-51s to slip up behind me. Sitting on my tail, one to the left, the other to the right, they had me completely boxed in. Whichever way I turned, I was for it. I tried to climb away to the right. It was the move the enemy pilot on that side had been waiting for.

His fire must have hit my coolant system, for I immediately started to trail a long thin banner of white vapour. The fate of my lovely Gustav was sealed.

I knew that I had to get out as quickly as possible. But I needed at least 250 metres of altitude to allow my parachute to open properly. The question was, would the engine hold out long enough for me to reach that height? And heaven be praised, it did. When I judged I was high enough to be safe, I began to go through the bale-out procedure. It was a routine I had practised dozens of times during training and gone over in my mind on countless occasions before dropping off to sleep: close the throttle, snap the helmet's R/T lead, undo seat harness, unlock and jettison cockpit canopy, let go of stick, push up, roll over cockpit sill to either left or right, wait, pull grip to open parachute. All went like clockwork until I got to the bit about letting go of stick. The moment I did so, I paid the penalty for yesterday's foolhardiness in not having that rudder trim fixed at Perugia.

The machine instantly fell away viciously to the left, trapping my booted feet beneath the instrument panel. Due to the strong negative g forces, I was completely unable to move my legs to free them. With the upper half of my body hanging out of the cockpit, I had only a few seconds to get the aircraft under control again. With a strength born of desperation I battled against the 180 km/h slipstream – this is the minimum speed at which an Me 109 could be held in the air without stalling, but is the equivalent of a ground wind strong enough to uproot trees – and somehow managed to slide back down into my seat.

I regained some of the height I had lost and tried again. But the second attempt was as unsuccessful as the first. Finally, at the third try, I made it. This time the sudden rush of air as I heaved myself up from the seat pulled me bodily out of my fur-lined flying boots. I could swear it sounded like a couple of champagne corks popping, and I can still clearly see my two boots as they whirled around my head. Then the force of the slipstream hit me like a ton-weight cushion and sent me somersaulting through the air.

Instinctively I pulled my 'chute release. In the few seconds it took for the parachute to open fully, I watched the ground below come rushing up towards me. Every detail, including the wavelets rippling the surface of a small lake, was so sharp – and growing in size so terrifyingly quickly – that it was like looking through the zoom lens of a camera. Convinced that the parachute was not going to open in time and that my last moments had come, my thoughts automatically turned to my family. But the 'Boandlkramer' – Bavaria's 'old man with the scythe' – was not quite ready for me yet. I felt the sudden jerk as the 'chute finally opened and, almost immediately afterwards, was drenched by a fountain of water as I landed with a colossal splash in the small lake. Miraculously, or so it seemed to me, I had gone from virtual free fall and near certain death to standing on my own two feet, up to my chest in water, all in the blink of an eye.

Incidentally, it was only many years later that I discovered – thanks to research carried out by the eminent British aviation historian Chris Goss and his contacts in America – that our opponents on this 6 April had not been RAF Mustangs at all, but P-39 Airacobras of the United States 12th Air Force... so much for those hours spent poring over aircraft recognition charts. The combat reports filed by pilots of the 350th Fighter Group operating out of Corsica on this date appear to leave very little room for doubt. They had been briefed to skip bomb rail and road bridges to the south of Grosseto and describe encountering Me 109 (and Fw 190) fighters, which dropped their belly tanks and attacked them in a shallow dive. The P-39s were jumped just as they were pulling up after delivering their bombs and didn't get the chance to regroup. The engagement dissolved into a series of individual dogfights – 'it was every man on his own, with most of the combat taking place down on the deck'.

Standing in my small Italian lake, it was totally immaterial to me at the time who had shot me down. I had more pressing matters to attend to – the recovery of Luftwaffe property, for a start. This was something else that had been drummed into us during training: never abandon items of equipment vital to the war effort. First my parachute, which, driven by the light breeze, was tugging me gently but insistently through the water. Although the metal release disc was just below the surface, I had no difficulty in twisting it and giving it a good hard thump to open it. Disentangling myself from the wet harness was slightly more of a problem, but I managed it in the end and gathered the folds of the 'chute together into as small a bundle as possible before slinging it over my left shoulder.

The feel of the sandy bed of the lake beneath my stockinged feet then reminded me of my flying boots; or rather the lack of them. I gazed around and was relieved to see them both floating, half submerged, some distance away. I waded out into deeper water to retrieve them, fished them out and clamped them under my right arm. At least I wouldn't now have to return to base minus my official footwear. It was well known that the Gruppenkommandeur had a bit of a thing about flying boots. He had even added what almost amounted to a private rider of his own to Luftwaffe regulations by decreeing that boots were always to be tied firmly below the knee. This was to prevent them from flying off when a pilot baled out. It was a sensible enough measure as far as it went, but I was mightily glad that I had not observed the rules – otherwise I might still be trapped by the feet beneath that instrument panel.

Having snapped the R/T lead in two before baling out, I was

still wearing my lightweight flying helmet. So that was about it. The last and most important item of equipment entrusted to me I could do nothing about. My poor Gustav had also come down in the shallow lake. But it must have bored itself deep into the sand, for all I could see was its tail sticking up above the surface, surrounded by a cloud of steam and smoke.

My next priority was to find some sign of life. The nearest dry land was only about fifty metres away where a row of tall poplars lined the bank behind the thick belt of reeds that fringed the lake. And beyond the poplars I could make out a pale grey column of smoke curling up into the blue sky above. I began to breast my way through the water towards the shore. The bed of the lake was very uneven and I kept stumbling into deep channels. Every time I did so, the water closed over my head. But despite these frequent duckings I retained an iron grip on the items of state property that I had so dutifully retrieved. As I neared the reeds the water grew shallower and I waded the last few metres through a thick green soup of algae and assorted underwater flora.

Climbing the bank on to terra firma, I made my way through the bushes between the poplars and there found a lush green meadow, bathed in sunlight, sloping upwards in front of me. At its far end stood a small farmhouse, whose chimney was the source of the smoke I had sighted earlier. After what I had just been through, it was picture of utter peace and tranquillity.

Standing in front of the house, lined up as if for inspection, was an entire Italian family: grandfather, grandmother, mama, papa and five bambini. They were all motionless and staring fixedly in the direction of the lake. The moment they clapped eyes on me, however, they fell to their knees as one. Raising their arms to the heavens, they began to sway rhythmically back and forth, loudly intoning what was obviously some Italian prayer or other. I caught the words 'Santa Madonna Maria' being repeated over and over again.

Still in a mild state of shock after the recent 'Mahalla' – our expression for a large dogfight – and fearing some nasty new surprise, I looked over my shoulder to see what had terrified them so. But there was nothing. Then it dawned on me – *I* was the nasty surprise! Their tiny little corner of the world had been practically untouched by the war so far. But today it had descended on them in all its fury. More than thirty fighter aircraft had thundered and roared just above their heads. Dozens of guns had hammered and barked, spitting death and destruction and shattering the calm of their everyday existence.

And then, as if from out of nowhere, one of the machines had appeared from behind the row of poplars at the bottom of their field and climbed steeply into the sky with an ear-splitting noise. The sound of the engine had suddenly died; the machine had tipped on to its side and, with a muffled 'whoomph', had dived straight into their lake, sending up fountains of earth and water. True, they later managed to explain to me, they had seen a figure leave the aircraft as it hung for a moment in the air before toppling over. But because of the high row of trees, they had not seen the parachute open at the very last moment. In their minds the pilot was undoubtedly dead.

A ghostly silence had descended as the aircraft all vanished as suddenly as they had appeared. Then they heard splashing noises coming from the lake. Moments later an apparition appeared from between the poplars – an unearthly figure with wide staring eyes, hair plastered to its forehead, dripping water, covered in green slime and long trailing tendrils, and half hidden in a white shroud. Unaware of the impression I had made, I trudged unconcernedly up the field, making for the white-haired grandfather, who was at the right-hand end of the row of kneeling, swaying supplicants. The closer I got to him, the closer his nose got to the ground and the more muffled his prayers became. Then I was standing right in front of him. He looked up at me wide-eyed. I indicated my muddy legs and said in my most elegant, if limited Italian, "Aqua Prego".

My polite request for water had an astonishing effect. Realizing that I was only human after all, the 'Santa Madonna Marias' ceased as if by magic. The whole family scrambled to its feet and surrounded me chattering excitedly. I was led to a bench standing against the white-painted wall of the house. While I relaxed in the reflected warmth of the sun, the eldest boy fetched a bucket of water and began to wash the mud off me. One of the girls picked the wet weeds from my flying overalls and dried me down. Another brought me a thick blanket. The farmer's wife placed a loaf of freshly baked white bread, a plate of smoked ham and a pitcher of the local red wine on the scrubbed wooden table in front of me.

I needed no second bidding and can only say – may my wife forgive me – that it was the best bite to eat I have ever had in my life. Despite the language difficulties, we all got along like a house on fire. "Dove in Germania?" the farmer's wife enquired, wanting to know where I lived in Germany. "Rosenheim in Bavaria – Baviera", my reply was mangled but clearly understood. "Ah, si, Baviera. And pictures of your mama and papa?" "Unfortunately, they're at the bottom of the lake – in the water – aqua." "Oh, scusi."

After a while our conversation was interrupted by the sound of a horse's hooves. It was the mayor of the local district in a two-wheeled gig. He had kindly come to offer me a lift to the military commandant's office in Grosseto. After a lengthy and emotional round of goodbyes, with lots of 'mille grazies' on my part, we finally set off. On the way we picked up Peter Ullmann, who had also baled out uninjured and had anxiously watched my desperate attempts to escape from my machine while descending in his parachute.

At Grosseto we found the commandant trying to get through to the Staffel at Canino to have us picked up. In the meantime Leutnant Schorsch Schneider and Unteroffizier Willi Lang had also been brought in. Both had claimed an enemy fighter apiece during the recent dogfight before they themselves had been shot down. Willi was unwounded, but we got a local doctor to have a look at Schorsch's wrist.

The four of us then spent the rest of the afternoon in one of the town's hotels. Having been told that it would take a good six hours to get from Canino to Grosseto by road, we were delighted to accept the mayor's invitation to dinner at his home that evening; in appreciation, as he put it, for our 'saving his town' from the enemy bombers. The lady of the house served up a delicious Italian meal accompanied by red wine, more red wine and – after she had discreetly withdrawn – yet more red wine.

At this point a quick change of scene to Canino, as subsequently recounted to me by the late Hans Eisen, a member of the Staffel: "Eisen!!!" "Jawoll, Herr Hauptmann!" "Select four men, grab yourselves machine-pistols, drive up to Grosseto as fast as you can and get our comrades out of there!!"

What had happened, apparently, was that the commandant's message had arrived at Canino completely garbled and our Staffelkapitän, Hauptmann Schröder, had understood it to mean that we were missing, presumed captured by the wicked partisans. Instead, after scouring Grosseto, our intrepid rescue party had eventually tracked us down late in the evening still at the mayor's house, high as kites, brimming over with brotherly love and serenading each other with German and Italian songs.

The next morning, after taking our lightly wounded companion to the Luftwaffe hospital at nearby Aquapendente, the three of us set off by train back to Aix-en-Provence. On the way we pulled off a stroke that I am sure will be familiar to many of the old soldiers who criss-crossed Europe on travel warrants during the war years. At Ventimiglia-Menton station on the French frontier we discovered that the French franc was worth a lot more on the black market than it was at the official rate of exchange.

So we pooled all our Italian lire and one of us, armed with his travel documents – which authorized the exchange of monies at any border crossing point on his stipulated route – changed our collective pot of Italian lire into French francs at the official rate. Then he exchanged it all back again into lire on the black market at a considerable profit. The other two then followed the same procedure, further adding to our growing bankroll each time. With our pockets fairly bulging with lire we continued on our way to Aix, where we convinced the paymaster that we had just flown in from Italy and requested that he exchange our Italian money for French, which he did in all good faith. We didn't make a huge fortune, of course, but we got a great deal of satisfaction from our little ploy; chalking it up as a victory for the little man, who had gathered a few crumbs from the table of world events.

At Aix I was finally assigned to 3./JG 2, now commanded after Hauptmann Sommer's untimely loss by Leutnant Clemens Walterscheid. Like every other newcomer to a front-line Staffel, irrespective of rank, I first had to fly as Katschmarek, or wing-man, to one of the unit's experienced pilots. It my case this was a veteran NCO. It seemed only natural to be briefed by him prior to take-off, to obey his instructions in the air, report back to him after landing and accept any advice or criticism he had to offer. As his superior in rank, I wasn't expected to stand to attention in front of him, of course. But operational units didn't go in for a lot of bullshit and heel-clicking during their daily routine anyway. Respect for a superior officer was automatically reflected in everybody's speech and bearing.

I was delighted to find that 3. Staffel had already been re-equipped with the Focke-Wulf Fw 190A-8. We spent the remainder of April flying almost daily patrols over that stretch of the Mediterranean separating the coast of southern France from the enemy-held island of Corsica. For those members of the Staffel who had previously been in action over the English Channel, these flights were regarded as little more than a welcome form of rest and recuperation affording them a chance to unwind. But for a relative tyro like myself, the knowledge alone that I was now playing a part in the real war on a day-to-day basis gave them a wholly different meaning.

Admittedly, there weren't many signs of the war in our particular backwater at this time, but I could never be sure in advance whether or not one of our peaceful forays out over the Mediterranean was going to result in contact with the enemy. In Italy I had been thrust into a combat situation suddenly and without any prior warning. Here I had to get used to a whole new range of emotions, from the involuntary tightness in the stomach when waking in the morning and prior to every take-off, to the wonderful sense of relief after the last landing of the day. In the event, we didn't encounter a single enemy aircraft during our entire three weeks of patrolling. I can only assume that with invasion looming in the north, and signs of an imminent breakout from the Anzio bridgehead in the south, the allies were all busy elsewhere.

The only untoward incident during this period occurred when we were returning from another fruitless patrol, flying at an altitude of about 8,000 metres, and my propeller decided for some reason to feather itself. As the engine died I jabbed at the pitch control thumbswitch on the throttle, but it had absolutely no effect. It looked as if I was going down, like it or not. Fortunately it was another glorious day. The sea was calm and the line of hills marking the French coast was already visible off to the right not too far ahead of me. Offering less wind resistance, a feathered propeller greatly increased an aircraft's glide capabilities, so I was fairly sure that I could reach the coast from this height.

But once I got there I would be faced with three choices. Should I try to ditch in shallow water, have another go at perfecting my parachuting skills – or attempt to get over the hills in the hope of finding a suitable spot for a belly landing? My three companions – we had been patrolling in Schwarm strength – had noticed at once what was wrong with my machine and were keeping close by me as I slowly began to lose height.

First I checked my overwater emergency equipment: life jacket, inflatable dinghy, bag of dye (to mark my position in the sea), flare pistol and cartridges in the bandolier strapped below my right knee. All present and correct. The more I thought about it, however, the less appealing my first two options became. The third didn't exactly fill me with enthusiasm either, but I decided to give it a go. I had sufficient height and speed in hand to cross the coastal hills comfortably and there, just beyond the ridge line, wonder of wonders, was a high valley, whose mix of green meadows and ploughed fields seemed ideally suited to the purpose I had in mind.

Unfortunately, the valley stretched from east to west, in other words, at right angles to my line of flight, and I was approaching its western end where stood a farmhouse and windmill surrounded by some large trees. To be on the safe side, I wanted to make use of the whole length of the valley, so I stood the Focke-Wulf on its left wing – I still had more than enough speed – executed a steep 270 degree turn between house and windmill, and swooped down towards the floor of the valley.

The propeller had come to a stop with one blade pointing

vertically upwards and the other two angled down to either side. As soon as I touched the ground the two lower blades were bent backwards to form a perfect pair of landing skids. Due to my still relatively high speed they bounced me briefly back into the air. And luckily so, for I neatly hurdled a deep, four-metre wide drainage ditch that I hadn't noticed before. Hitting the ground again, I ploughed my own lengthy furrow down the valley before finally coming to a stop. I jumped out on to the wing of my machine and waved up at my comrades circling above. Seeing that I was unhurt, they waggled their own wings before heading off back to base.

Not far from where I stood a farmer had been working with some female field hands. Although naturally a bit taken aback at the manner of my arrival, they hurried across for a closer look at their unexpected visitor. As my French was far better than my Italian, we were soon deep in friendly conversation; helped along no doubt by my offering cigarettes to the farmer and handing round my tin of 'Schokakola' – containing triangular segments of concentrated chocolate; part of our flight rations – to the girls, and accepting liberal quantities of home-made red wine in return.

After about four hours the unit's recovery crew turned up in their truck. As my machine was being hoisted aboard by crane, several hundredweight of earth and stones poured out of its wheel wells. Once it was secured, and the NCO in charge of the crew had presented the farmer with a form guaranteeing that he would be reimbursed for all damage done to his property and land, we slowly set off back to Aix. Upon inspection it was found that my crate required very little repair. As the engine had stopped before the belly landing, it had suffered no serious damage. All that needed to be done was to fit a replacement propeller and clean up the airframe. After just four days I got it back as good as new.

As a break from our routine Mediterranean patrolling, the pilots of the 190 Staffel – that was us – were flown to Berlin in a Ju 52. As we were approaching to land at the capital's Tempelhof airport, an unexpected sight met our eyes. Just in front of us, flying between the clouds of smoke still lingering in the air from a recent American bombing raid, was a bright red Focke-Wulf Fw 200 Condor. Someone suggested that it could be a civil airliner arriving from a neutral country, possibly from Stockholm in Sweden. That had to be the case, although we were amazed that scheduled civilian airline services were still operating over Germany in the fifth year of total war.

After landing in Berlin we were taken to the Focke-Wulf factory at Aschersleben on the northern edge of the Harz mountains. We were to collect a batch of new Fw 190A-8s and ferry them back to Aix, where they would be used re-equip my old 4. Staffel. Due to my previous experience as an instructor, I was one of several pilots selected to help 4./JG 2 transition from its Me 109G-6s on to the radial-engined Focke-Wulfs.

But it wasn't to be simply a case of showing them where all the taps and levers were and then sending them on their merry way. Some desk-bound psychologist or morale booster with too much time on his hands had formulated a special procedure designed to strengthen the bond between an individual pilot and his machine. From now on a pilot wasn't just pointed towards a new aircraft and told to get on with it. It was to be ceremoniously handed over to him in person by his Kommandeur, who would also present him with a certificate of ownership recording the name of the pilot, the markings carried by the machine and its serial number.

This all struck us as being a bit too artificial and overly theatrical. The traditional relationship between man and machine, where we regarded the aircraft we flew almost as a kind of reliable mate, had served us well enough in the past. It was much more natural and far more binding than any fancy scrap of paper.

This irrelevant nonsense was just one more sign of the changing times. Another had been the appointment some time earlier of a unit NS-Führungsoffizier, or 'National-Socialist leadership officer'. It had been decreed from on high that every Geschwader was to select one of its members to perform this role, which was roughly the equivalent of a political commissar in the Red Army. His job would be to keep us informed of all the latest political developments and ensure that we toed the party line, even though none of us was actually allowed to join the Party – not that we particularly wanted to, I hasten to add.

JG 2 had not escaped this blanket order but, typically, did not choose a '150 per center' for the post. This was the term commonly used to describe a fanatical, dyed-in-the-wool Nazi and, as far as I am aware, there were no such individuals in the Geschwader's ranks anyway. In fact, during my whole time in the Luftwaffe I can only recall ever meeting one example of the type, and that was an Oberleutnant from Austria.

The unfortunate selected to be JG 2's NS-Führungsoffizier was totally unsuited to the part. This meant we were not bothered by such matters and were left alone in peace and quiet and ignorance. I can only hope that those members of the Geschwader who were captured with him at the end of the war stood up for him during the 'denazification' process by informing their interrogators that his political activities, such as they were, had been foisted on him and were not a matter of personal conviction.

In fact, the difference between our own morale and party ideology could not have been greater. It was displayed by our openly telling political jokes of the most scurrilous nature. On one occasion the duty officer did his hilarious impression of a Goebbel's speech, mimicking the propaganda minister's voice and style to perfection, but talking the most ridiculous and slanderous rubbish. And this was not just to a group of close friends, either – but over the camp's P/A system, so that his words could be heard blaring out from loudspeakers all over the airfield.

On 1 May 1944 all four Staffeln of I. Gruppe were transferred back up to JG 2's traditional areas of operation between Paris and the Channel coast. This had been the Geschwader's field of activity ever since the end of the French campaign in the early summer of 1940. Originally its component units had been based on a string of airfields right on the coast stretching from Dieppe down to Cherbourg and beyond. But over the intervening four years they had gradually been pushed back further and further inland by the continually growing might of the allies.

By the time of my arrival from the south of France with the rest of I. Gruppe, JG 2's forward landing grounds were situated roughly along the line Amiens-Le Mans. Our exact destination was Cormeilles, near Pontoise to the northwest of Paris and less than ten kilometres from the Geschwaderstab at Marines. For the next fortnight or so we would fly on average two or three missions a day, mainly against marauding Jabos, or allied fighter-bombers. But we were also sent up against the Americans' heavy bomber formations. And these were to prove much more of a problem.

When they first encountered American four-engined 'heavies', the Luftwaffe's fighter pilots in the west had followed the long held theory and attacked from the rear. But in practice this tactic was quickly found to be both ineffective and costly. While intent on the laborious business of slowly overhauling the bombers from astern, the German pilots not only ran the risk of attack from the enemy fighter escort, they also had to face the bombers' own massed defensive fire, which was heaviest to

119

the rear.

It was our own late Kommodore, Oberstleutnant Egon Mayer – 'Kanalmayer' – who came up with a possible but radical solution: the frontal attack. Admittedly, this required strong nerves and lightning-fast reactions, but it did away with the long and dangerous stern chase. The bombers' only fully forward-firing armament was in the nose and upper turret. The gunners would first see the fast approaching fighters as tiny dots and hardly have time to take aim before their attackers were upon them and gone.

For the fighter pilots, approaching in a high-speed shallow dive, the situation was far more favourable. A bomber's huge wingspan of more than thirty metres made it a feasible target from a range of about 700 metres out. At a combined closing speed of very nearly 1,000 km/h, or 277 metres per second, the fighter thus had a good two seconds of firing time, although the last split second of this had to be held in reserve for breaking away beneath the bomber formation.

The fundamental difficulty in this method of attack was in getting the fighter force into position far enough ahead of the target to allow a frontal assault to be carried out without being spotted and attacked by the bombers' own escorting fighters while in the process. And by the time I arrived at the front such room for manoeuvre no longer existed. Aware of our methods, the Americans had provided their bombers with a strong forward fighter screen specifically to counter such frontal attacks. As a result we had to amend our own tactics accordingly. Now we would approach the bombers at maximum speed from diagonally ahead, rake the formation's flanks with our fire as we passed in a curving dive, and then get the hell out. Our official R/T codeword for this latter action was 'verreisen', which meant literally 'to go on a journey' or 'to travel'. The Gruppe managed to claim several successes with this method, but not enough to

Datum	Flugzeug	i-Zeit	Flug-dauer	Höhe	Wind-richtung und Stärke	Gelände	Startart (G, A, W, F)	Bemerkungen, Prüfungen Eintragungen des Flugleiters
11.11.31	Grunau	R				Jne Dorf	G	
11.11.31	„	R 6				Annilz	„	
8.9.38	Zögling 33	R				Unter-Adelsdorf	G	
15.9.38	„ „	6				Jakobsberg	G	
6.10.38	Grunau	21				Jakobsberg	G	1. A
„	„ „	16				„	G	
„ „	„ „	20				„	G	2. A
„ „	„ „	20				„	G	3. A
„ „	„ „	21				„	G	4. A
30.10.38	„ „	31				„	G	Anfang
1.11.38	„ „	5				„	G	
„ „	„ „	25				Hanisferding	G	5. A
11.11.38	Zögling	18				Jakobsberg	G	
16.11.38	„	17	19/130			„	G	
16.11.38	„	83	17/130					
1.11.38	„		59	12				

Startart: G=Gummiseil, A=Auto, W=Winden-, F=Flugzeugschlepp

Above left: The first page of the author's glider pilot's logbook marking his first flight in the Grunau G9 on 7 November 1937. Note the 'R' in column four indicating that it was just a 'Rutsch', or slide along the ground. By flight number ten (see 30 October 1938) he was staying in the air for all of thirty-one seconds. The 'Gs' in column six show that every take-off was a catapult launch by 'gummiseil', or rubber bungee cord.

Above right: The cover of the author's NSFK (National-Socialist Flying Corps) glider pilot's licence.

Nationalsozialistisches Fliegerkorps (NSFK)

Deutscher Gleitflieger-Ausweis — B —

Nr. 35285

Left: The notorious Grunau G9 'skull-splitter' glider. Here the wooden brace in front of the pilot's face has at least been bound with tape to offer a modicum of protection against concussion in the event of a heavy landing.

left: Family and friends at Thansau, 1935. The au- (standing right) with, from the left: Frau Schloss- an, the author's sister Rada, his mother, and Edith lossmann.

right: In the mid-'thirties most air-minded German ths began by building and flying model aircraft.

Top: The author's father, wearing Bavarian national costume, photographed on the Schlossmann family's Hubertus farm estate in Transvaal, South Africa, in 1938.

Above left: The annual Deutschlandflug, or round-Germany air rally, was a major attraction involving all kinds of aircraft and drawing huge crowds.

Above right: One of the decidedly anti-Nazi political cartoons sent home by the author's father during his time in South Africa.

Left: The rubber bungee cord falls away as this Grunau Baby glider takes cleanly to the air from a steep hillside.

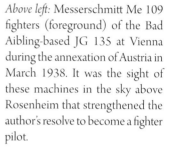

Above left: Messerschmitt Me 109 fighters (foreground) of the Bad Aibling-based JG 135 at Vienna during the annexation of Austria in March 1938. It was the sight of these machines in the sky above Rosenheim that strengthened the author's resolve to become a fighter pilot.

Above right: A Dornier Do 17P long-range reconnaissance aircraft of the type flown by the Fernaufklärungsgruppe/Ob.d.L.

Middle: Like all new recruits, the author had to swear an oath of allegiance upon joining the Luftwaffe.

Bottom Left: The portly figure of Generalfeldmarschall Hugo Sperrle, the AOC of Air Fleet 3, about to board his personal Junkers Ju 52 transport aircraft.

Top: At the start of the Battle of Britain Villacoublay airfield hou all 100-plus Heinkel He 111 bombers of Kampfgeschwader 55. Th machines belong to III. Gruppe.

Above left: There was a darker undercurrent to life in Paris. German male personnel, whether military or civilian, were not permitted to w der the streets on their own. They always had to go out in groups of th or more, preferably with male escorts. These female auxiliaries – 'so grises' ('grey mice') to the Parisians – are visiting the Place de l'Opé

Above right: By the winter of 1940/41 only the aircraft of Geschwaderstab (wing HQ) and III./KG 55 remained at Villac blay. Wearing provisional night camouflage, this machine is read for another nocturnal mission.

Left: The author (second right) and friends go sightseeing in Pari

Top left: The Easter 1941 issue of the German troops' guide to 'What's On in Paris'. On the back cover it suggests that the nightclub to visit is the 'Shéhérazade' at 3 Rue de Liège. Having followed the magazine's advice ...

Top right: ... these officers and their ladies appear to be thoroughly enjoying one of the establishment's main attractions.

Bottom left: Pre-flight discussion at Luftkriegsschule 4, Fürstenfeldbruck, 1942. The author is on the left with Focke-Wulf Fw 44 trainer behind.

Bottom right: Physical training during the NCOs' instructional course at Neukuhren in the summer of 1941; the author at centre right.

promoting the author to the rank of Leutnant as of 1 November 1942 ...

Above: ... and the portrait taken to mark the event.

Top left: A Bücker Bü 131 Jungmann sports and trainer aircraft. This particular example was operated by the Luftdienstkommando, the Luftwaffe's Air Service Command.

Top right: 'In the name of the Führer ...' the official document, with Göring's signature at the bottom,

Middle left: Morning parade outside JG 107's ski chalet at Zug in the Austrian Alps.

Above left: A Wehrmacht military band gives an outdoor concert on the Champs Elysées in the spring of 1941.

Top left: The Heinkel He 51, the Luftwaffe's standard first-line fighter of the mid-'thirties, made a rugged training machine during the war years.

Top right: A 'Rotte', or pair, of Arado Ar 96 advanced trainers.

Above left: The sleek Arado Ar 96 advanced trainer, whose retractable undercarriage was very nearly the author's undoing.

Above right: The author demonstrating how it's done – without the benefit of skis! – Zug, February 1943.

Right: Hauptmann Adalbert Sommer, the Staffelkapitän of 3./JG 107 at Nancy-Essay.

Below left: From Nancy the author followed the line of the River Meuse northwest to the battlefields of World War I to commemorate the first anniversary of his father's death.

*Below right:*Not all of Nancy was as attractive as the old town area. But although this giant slagheap on the outskirts was undoubtedly an eyesore, it proved a very useful landmark in bad weather.

*Bottom:*The Me 109's notoriously weak, narrow-tracked undercarriage was the cause of many ground accidents. This machine's port mainwheel leg has partially collapsed and its fairing has been snapped in two.

Above left: Messerschmitt Me 109D fighter-trainers.

Above right: A Messerschmitt Me 109 makes a firing pass at a ground target during gunnery practice.

Middle left: A Messerschmitt Me 109E fighter-trainer taxies out prior to take-off.

Bottom left: A late-war Messerschmitt Me 109G fighter-trainer in flight.

Above left: The author's newfound 'bosom friend', Leutnant Stefan Marinopolski, later flew Me 109Gs with the Bulgarian air force's 6th Fighter Wing.

Above right: The ex-French air force Dewoitine D.520 fighter was the one aircraft that the author actively disliked.

Right: A North American NAA-64, originally ordered by the French air force as a two-seat trainer, in service with 3./JG 107 at Nancy-Essay in the spring of 1943.

Below right: Due to its extremely short take-off and landing capabilities, the Fieseler Fi 156 'Storch' light communications aircraft was popular with Luftwaffe units in France as a general runabout. This particular example has put down in the Place de la Concorde in the very heart of Paris.

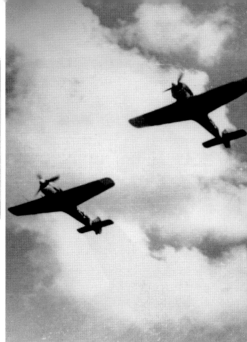

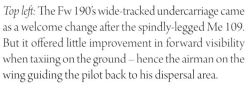

Top left: The Fw 190's wide-tracked undercarriage came as a welcome change after the spindly-legged Me 109. But it offered little improvement in forward visibility when taxiing on the ground – hence the airman on the wing guiding the pilot back to his dispersal area.

Top right: A pair of Focke-Wulf Fw 190s flying a perfect Rotte formation with the leader on the right.

Above left: Two pairs made up a Schwarm, with the leaders in the middle.

Right: Hajo Herrmann, the originator of the 'Wilde Sau' concept, pictured here as an Oberst and wearing the Oak Leaves with Swords awarded to him in January 1944.

Top left: An Fw 190 Wilde Sau night-fighter pilot prepares for a nocturnal sortie.

Top right: The author, right, with Peter Ullmann in Genoa, Italy, in April 1944.

Above left: The Geschwaderkommodore of JG 2, Egon Mayer, seen here as a Major, was credited with developing the frontal method of attack against American heavy bombers. He was killed in action on 2 March 1944.

Above right: A Halifax bomber of the RAF silhouetted against clouds illuminated by searchlights from below.

Above left: A Rotte of Fw 190s sets off on another uneventful patrol of the Mediterranean coast.

Above right: To help pilots judge the distance when carrying out a frontal attack on a heavy bomber, JG 2 set up a Revi gunsight (foreground) with a large-scale model of an American Flying Fortress in front of it.

Left: Pilots of I./JG 2 snatch a cigarette break between missions in northern France.

Below: Luftwaffe fighters in Normandy had to be kept hidden away under trees out of sight of prowling allied fighter-bombers.

Top: Major Erich Hohagen (left) was the Kommandeur of I./JG 2 during the author's time with the Gruppe.

Above left: Oberstleutnant Kurt Bühligen served as Geschwaderkommodore of JG 2 from just prior to D-Day until the end of the war.

Above right: The Focke-Wulfs suffered increasing attrition as D-Day approached. This one is going down after being hit in the starboard wing root.

...ve: Belated birthday boy Leutnant Siegfried
...ke proudly displaying the Knight's Cross
...he won a week after D-Day.

...ve right: Early on the morning of D-Day, 6
...1944, the near deserted streets of Nancy
...ped to the sounds of cars and motorcycles
...g around gathering up the pilots of I./JG

...dle: A Focke-Wulf Fw 190 fighter fitted
...underwing rocket launchers.

...om right: Ground crew load a 21cm rocket
...a Focke-Wulf's underwing launch tube.

Top left: Hauptmann Josef Wurmheller (left) led the rocket attack on allied invasion shipping off Gold Beach on the morning of D-Day.

Top right: Post-war Munich showing damage to the canopied roof of the main railway station in the foreground and the twin spires of the city's famous Frauenkirche beyond.

Above left: British armour heads inland from Gold Beach. The author came down in his parachute to the left of the road leading up from the beach in the background.

Above right: The author visits the spot some fifty years later.

Left: The author's Certificate of Discharge marking the end of more than six-and-a-half years of military service.

make any great impact.

In mid-May we – 2. and 3. Staffeln, that is – were transferred to another forward landing ground some thirty kilometres to the north of Cormeilles. It was not a particularly well-chosen spot, for the main landing run was crossed by a country road. Although the ditches on either side of it had been filled in, slight depressions still remained and these, combined with the surface of the road itself, made for a very bumpy ride. In addition, two large trees had been left standing directly beneath the approach path. This meant that we had to perform what we called 'Californian giant slips' – a sort of exaggerated sideslip – in order to touch down as far in front of the road crossing as possible. That way we were able to bump across it at fairly slow speed and thus avoid damaging our aircraft.

Apart from this slight handicap, our new base was well nigh perfect. We were quartered in a small chateau near the village of Boissy-les-Bois, although I, like a number of other pilots, occupied a room in a private house in the village itself. The surroundings could only be described as extremely pleasant. An excellent cook kept us well fed, there was a convivial mess complete with the obligatory bar, and the chateau's gardens were a riot of late spring colour with the trees in blossom and many flower beds already in full bloom.

In fact, it had all the trappings of a luxury hotel – had it not been for the pervasive air of tension; the inescapable feeling of apprehension on waking every morning, not knowing what the day would bring. In the pilots' bus taking us out to the airstrip everybody was outwardly relaxed and full of horseplay, but inside each of us there was a small but insistent voice saying, "Will I be seeing these lads on the bus again tomorrow... or they me?" These feelings stayed with me for as long as I remained outside my aircraft, sitting in an easy chair reading, or perhaps playing a hand of cards with two or three of the other pilots.

I./JG 2's likely opponents in the action of 25 May were the
American 364th Fighter Group, who lost six of their
P-38 Lightnings on that date.

But the moment the order to scramble was broadcast over
the field's loudspeakers and the ground crews began to remove
the camouflage netting from the machines, push them from
their dispersal points hidden under the trees and help me to
strap myself into my seat, all other thoughts were forgotten and
it was time to concentrate solely on the coming mission. Once
in the air every pilot's full attention was focussed on the business in hand; keeping in contact with his Rotte or Schwarm
leader and constantly quartering the sky for the first signs of
the reported 'Indianer' or 'dicke Autos' – 'large cars'; multi-engined bombers. If we did make contact with the enemy, we

were almost invariably vastly outnumbered. We suffered the inevitable consequences and next morning another one or two familiar faces would be missing from the bus taking us out to the field.

The mission of 25 May was typical. We were scrambled to engage a formation of enemy bombers reported to be approaching our area. After a long climb we sighted them. In all truth, it would have been hard to miss them: a force of about 120 American B-24 Liberators, flying in four boxes of some thirty bombers each, escorted by at least fifty Lockheed P-38 Lightnings. In all, the enemy must have numbered well over 150. We were just five!

The Staffelkapitän was leading. I was tucked in on his left, with my Katschmarek alongside me (by this time I had been elevated to the position of a Rotte leader), while the other pair, the experienced Unteroffizier Paul Herbing and tyro Fähnrich Schiller, were a little way behind us acting as Holzaugen – literally 'wooden eyes' or lookouts. Their job was to guard our tails.

Leutnant Walterscheid manoeuvred us into an attacking position some way ahead, and off to one side of the bombers. In a long curving pass against the outer box of Liberators we were able to claim a 'Herausschuss'. This was a term peculiar to anti-bomber operations. Meaning a 'shooting out', it was used to describe a bomber damaged so severely that it was forced to drop out of formation. In the Luftwaffe's rather complicated points scoring system (used to determine the conferral of awards), a Herausschuss rated just below the total destruction of a bomber. For once it had left the safety of its combat box, a damaged bomber limping along on its own was regarded as a relatively easy target. And any pilot who subsequently chanced upon such a lone straggler and finally shot it down received fewer points than the original Herausschuss claimant.

After completing our single high-speed firing run it was time to make ourselves scarce. But to our amazement we spotted a small group of the escorting Lightnings that had apparently, and inexplicably, failed to notice that their charges were under attack. They were stooging along seemingly oblivious to all around them. It was a rare opportunity and one too good to miss. With the speed built up during our diving pass on the bombers, we were able to curve in behind the unsuspecting P-38s. Banking hard to the left, the Staffelkapitän claimed the two enemy fighters flying on the extreme right, while I put a burst of cannon fire into a third.

Its pilot immediately baled out and tumbled past beneath my wings like a badly wrapped parcel. I can only hope that he delayed opening his 'chute, for all this had taken place at an altitude of about 6,500 metres, and a slow descent by parachute from that height could well prove fatal, either from suffocation in the thin air or by freezing to death. The fourth Lightning had dived away. But we didn't chase after him as our Holzaugen were reporting the rapid approach of another gaggle of enemy fighters.

Instead, we stood our machines on their noses, rammed the throttles forward and in an instant had 950 km/h on the clock. Glancing back over my shoulder to make sure that all was well, I was horrified to see that Schiller, one of our two Holzaugen, had decided to stay upstairs and battle it out with four of the newly arrived Lightnings. But his experience didn't match his foolhardy courage, and two of the P-38s were already sliding unnoticed on to his tail.

I wrenched my Focke-Wulf out of its dive, intending to go to his aid. A zoom climb, plus a generous amount of boost, got me up above the Lightnings in very short order. But it was already too late. Even as I turned in towards the enemy pair, I knew that I would never get into position to open fire on them in time. In desperation I yelled at Schiller over the R/T: "Verreisen sie, verreisen sie!" – "Start travelling, start travelling!" – but he gave no indication of having heard me.

A second or two later I had another quartet of Lightnings sniffing at my own tail. With tracers flying past my ears, it was high time I took my own advice. I pushed the stick fully forward and went 'travelling' again in another almost vertical dive. With the needle jammed against the 950, I was relieved to find that none of the Lightnings had been able to follow me down. At 2,000 metres I attempted to pull out, but the stick was rock solid. Standing on the rudder pedals, I heaved on it with both hands, but it refused to budge. As a last resort I tried the tailplane trim switch. Thanks to the Focke-Wulf's electrical system, all it took was a flick of my little finger (in an Me 109 recovery from a dive like this would have been impossible).

The machine responded instantly, and with such brute strength and agility that I was pressed down into my seat with a g force the like of which I had never before experienced in my whole life. I couldn't even lift my finger from the trim switch. A dark veil, razored by flashes of lightning, descended before my eyes. But I remained semi-conscious throughout and was dimly aware of the aircraft flattening out. I regained full vision after another second or so to find myself about 1,000 metres off the ground, flying straight and level, and with the clock still hovering on the 800 mark.

A few hours after landing back at base we received news that our two Holzaugen had both been found dead in the wreckage of their machines. The loss of one had been particularly needless and could so easily have been avoided. How the other met his end we never did find out. There had been no witnesses.

There was a postscript to the action, however. My shouted warning to Schiller over the R/T had of course been heard over the Geschwader ops room speakers. As a result the Geschwaderkommodore, Oberstleutnant Kurt Bühligen – after talking the matter over with my Gruppenkommandeur, Major Erich Hohagen – decided to have me report in person at wing HQ to describe the events in full. For without knowing the true circumstances, my orders to Schiller to 'start travelling' could well have been construed as inciting a subordinate to display cowardice in the face of the enemy. But when I explained exactly what had taken place, I was completely exonerated.

This was the only occasion that I was to come into close contact with Oberstleutnant Bühligen. Although he had been appointed Geschwaderkommodore just a few days beforehand, he had served with JG 2 since the Battle of Britain; achieving his first victory as an Unteroffizier on 4 September 1940. He had since taken his total to very nearly a century, all scored against the Western allies, and was now wearing the Oak Leaves to his Knight's Cross. My lasting impression of him was that he was no hidebound military martinet, but someone who was both approachable and prepared to listen to both sides of an argument before forming a judgement.

My Gruppenkommandeur, incidentally, had also opened his score over southern England in the summer of 1940 (when a member of JG 51). Major Erich Hohagen struck me as being very correct, but always ready to stand up for those serving under him. His pet hate, I was told, was 'bumph' – he had an aversion to paperwork of any kind.

In addition to our operations over France, we were sometimes also called upon to participate in so-called 'Defence of the Reich' missions. On these occasions we would take off at first light and deploy to Trier, just over the German border. Here we were held at readiness until the enemy's intentions became clear, awaiting the order to scramble if the bomber stream was reported to be heading towards our region of southwest Germany. Now and again we would also land at Trier at the end of such missions in order to refuel before heading back to France. Once when we were just about to touch down at Trier, it was about 14.00hrs on a scorching hot May afternoon and our cockpits were like ovens, I spotted an enticingly blue body of water shimmering in the sun very close to the airfield.

I drew this pool to my Katschmarek's attention, indicating that we should park our machines on the perimeter of the field as close to it as possible and grab the chance for a refreshing swim. This we did, climbing first out of our crates, and then out of our sweat-soaked flying gear, before rushing across and plunging stark naked into the water. We were snorting and splashing about like a pair of happy porpoises when we heard an angry yell, 'what the devil did we think we were playing at, this was a reservoir supplying drinking water to the townspeople of Trier!' We obeyed the order to clear off at once. The quick dip had been wonderfully invigorating, all the same – and I never did hear of any epidemic of plague or pestilence breaking out among the good folk of Trier.

Our Defence of the Reich operations weren't crowned with much success. But one of them did end in my having to make another emergency landing. It was early morning and four of us were about twenty minutes into the flight to Trier. We were cruising along at a height of some 400 metres, following the northern bank of the River Aisne, when my engine emitted a loud bang and the RPM needle suddenly started to unwind. As was my custom, I had been scanning the terrain *en route*, keeping an eye open for possible forced-landing sites – after all, one could never be too sure. But they seemed to be few and far between in this region; in fact, it would be more accurate to say that there weren't any at all.

This stretch of the Aisne reminded me very much of the valley of the Moselle: deep, narrow and winding. Thick forests stretched away on either side, while crammed into the floor of the valley alongside the river itself were roads, railway tracks, buildings and all sorts of other awkward items, none of which was particularly conducive to a successful forced landing. Then I remembered a few minutes earlier seeing a small green clearing cut back into the forest from the lip of the gorge. I carefully reversed course and pushed the throttle fully forward to extract the last ounce of power out of the failing engine. I soon caught sight of the clearing again and executed a gentle turn to come in from across the river.

I was on my final approach for a wheels-up landing when the engine finally died altogether, but fortunately it was at the point where I was about to chop the throttle anyway. Now fully committed, I was horrified to discover that the clearing wasn't a clearing at all, but a fully mature orchard. But I had run out of options. I steered the Focke-Wulf down straight into the middle of the fruit trees. At least they would make for a softer landing than the thick trunks of the trees in the high forest that otherwise surrounded me on all sides. Even so, I couldn't shake the feeling of someone making his last journey to the executioner's block.

The armoured nose of my machine smashed into the luxuriant crowns of the fruit trees, sending leaves and branches flying in all directions. My left wing sliced a tree neatly in two. Then the right wing did the same, and then the left again. I progressed through the orchard, gradually sinking lower and leaving a lengthening trail of devastation in my wake, before emerging at the far end, only a couple of metres off the ground, and slamming down onto a small patch of grass separating what a moment ago had been the orderly rows of fruit trees from the start of the forest proper.

The jolt of the landing sprained my back slightly, but otherwise I was unhurt. My sturdy 190 had protected me well and I didn't have a scratch on me. But the machine itself was a total write-off. The fuselage was buckled and the surfaces of both wings displayed the kind of curves that any smart young lady of the time would have died for.

When smoke began to pour from the engine cowling I hopped quickly out, fearing the whole thing might explode at any moment. Luckily there was a flak observation tower nearby. From their eyrie the crew had enjoyed a bird's eye view as I carved my spectacular swathe of destruction through the orchard. They were soon on the scene. After helping me back to the tower, they rang the Staffel and looked after me royally until a car came to pick me up. Naturally, the matter didn't rest there. The reason for my forced landing had to be established. Subsequent investigation showed that the engine's rear mounting ring had broken, either as a result of poor materials or from metal fatigue, and so once again I was off the hook.

Despite – or perhaps because of – the burdens of war, we rarely passed up an opportunity to 'hang one on'. Whenever Saint Peter was kind enough to send down some nice thick clouds in the afternoon, and our 'weather frog', or meteorologist, predicted more of the same for the following day, our thoughts naturally turned to the best way of filling the unexpected free time. If neither we nor the Tommys were going to have to haul our backsides into the air early the next morning, it meant that the evening ahead was ours. Thus it came about that another of our many aces, Leutnant Siegfried Lemke, the Kapitän of 1. Staffel – who, with nearly forty victories to his credit, was already in line for the Knight's Cross – decided to devote one such evening to a belated birthday celebration. He generously invited four or five of us to join him in the festivities. These, however, were not to be held in the mess bar, our everyday watering hole. Thanks to the intervention of the aforementioned Saint Peter, Lemke had a much more exclusive venue in mind.

Somehow he had obtained permission to make use of the unit's 'Holzgaser', a converted civilian vehicle driven by a wood-burning contraption – technically known as a gasifier, I believe – mounted at the rear. It was in this unlikely conveyance that we duly set forth on the eighty-kilometre journey to Paris; more specifically, to one of the French capital's then hottest night spots – 'Les Doges' in the Rue des Italiens. It was a birthday party to remember. When the place started to empty towards midnight, we hired the three-man musical combo to stay on until four in the morning to play just for our enjoyment alone.

There was very nearly a disaster during the trip back to base in the cold light of dawn. Not because of the state we were in, which was admittedly decidedly merry, but due to a sudden encounter with a tractor being driven by a stouthearted son of the French soil, who clearly regarded the whole width of the road as his personal and rightful domain. It was thanks entirely to the incredibly fast reactions of our birthday boy at the wheel that we lived to fight another day... and what a day it would prove to be.

CHAPTER 7

THE NORMANDY INVASION

By the end of May 1944 talk was turning more and more to the subject of the coming invasion. We all knew that an allied landing somewhere along the Channel coast of France was imminent. That had been made perfectly clear to us a few days earlier when Major Hohagen had assembled the pilots of all four Staffeln together at Cormeilles to read out an 'Order of the Day' from Reichsmarschall Hermann Göring. The C-in-C informed us that the invasion was expected to take place some time in the next three weeks, and that the entire Luftwaffe stood poised and ready to oppose the landings in a battle that would, he said, decide the fate of Germany.

I also seem to recall his warning us that none of us could count on coming out of this battle alive. This didn't impress us all that much, as the odds we were already facing on a day-to-day basis made our prospects of survival in the longer term slightly less than rosy. But we derived some hope and comfort from the fact that the full Luftwaffe complement – or at least a substantial part of it – would be sent in to support us.

We knew from personal experience that the Luftwaffe's

ground organization across the whole of northern France had been built up to accommodate the sudden influx of several thousand aircraft. There were ample stocks of fuel, ammunition, spare parts and ration stores on every airfield and forward landing ground. We ourselves were certainly suffering no shortage of aviation fuel. We reckoned that this would give us, if not actual superiority, then at least parity with the enemy in the air for a good three or four days. During this crucial period we hoped to be able to ensure freedom of movement for our troops on the ground by protecting them against low-level attack from allied fighters and fighter-bombers. With its mobility thus guaranteed, the army would then be in a position to prepare and launch a massive counter-attack that would throw the invaders back into the sea. This was the plan. How different everything turned out to be in reality.

Over the weekend of 3 and 4 June the whole Geschwader was suddenly pulled out of northern France, the area it had been defending so vigorously for four long years. This move seemed completely unfathomable to us at the time. With hindsight I can only assume that our intelligence services had somehow got wind of the location, if not the exact date, of the coming landings, and that we had been withdrawn out of harm's way of the softening-up bombing strikes that could be expected to precede the invasion itself. Whatever the true reason, the redeployment saw Hauptmann Herbert Huppertz's III. Gruppe depart for the French Atlantic coast, while II. Gruppe, commanded now by my erstwhile Staffelkapitän, Hauptmann Georg Schröder, retired to Germany by road and rail to collect a fresh batch of Me 109Gs.

In the meantime, we of I./JG 2 had been ordered to Nancy in eastern France. I was no stranger to this part of the world, of course, having spent many happy months there while serving with JG 107. But we were not to occupy the main Nancy-Essay

132

airfield. We were directed instead to makeshift landing strips outside the town; 1. and 3. Staffeln being assigned a large meadow up on the nearby plateau. (JG 107, incidentally, had vacated Nancy-Essay less than a month earlier. After a heavy bombing raid on the field by Flying Fortresses late in April caused widespread damage, Old Frau Meyer had led his chicks back to Markersdorf in eastern Germany.) Upon our arrival at Nancy we found that rooms had been reserved for us in a number of hotels and guesthouses in the town, where we whiled away the remainder of the weekend and the Monday in complete inactivity.

Our peace was rudely shattered around 5am on the morning of Tuesday, 6 June, by the sounds of cars and motorcycles racing through the streets of Nancy rounding up the Gruppe's pilots from their individual billets. A motorcyclist screeched to a halt in front of my hotel, yelled my name and the single word, "Invasion!" I was out on the street in no time flat and he quickly drove me up to the plateau. By 6am we were taking off through the knee-high grass and heading back in the direction of Paris, our exact destination being the airfield at Creil, some forty-five kilometres NNE of the city.

Here we were informed that our Focke-Wulfs were to be fitted with rockets. While the armourers began the two-hour job of attaching the launch tubes beneath the wings of our fighters, we set about learning how to fire our lethal new toys. The 21-cm rocket-powered mortar had originally been developed for use by the ground forces. The army tried to disguise its true function by christening it the 'Nebelwerfer,' or 'smoke discharger'. But the allied troops who found themselves on the receiving end of a salvo of these banshee-wailing missiles soon found other names for them; 'Moaning Minnies' and 'Screaming Meemies' being among the more repeatable.

The Nebelwerfer was then modified as an air-to-air weapon

for the Luftwaffe under the designation 21-cm BR (for Bor-drakete, or airborne rocket), although it was commonly referred to simply as the 'Dödel', a generic name – something along the lines of a 'thingummy' – that we applied to all kinds of items, including the Knight's Cross. It had first been used against the Americans' heavy bombers in the summer of 1943. With a max-imum range of at least 2,000 metres, it could be launched from well outside the effective range of the bombers' defensive fire and the first Luftwaffe Gruppen to employ it operationally were said to have achieved considerable success. But it was one thing simply to lob a rocket into the middle of a big box of tightly packed bombers. We were told that we were going to have to use it against the allies' invasion shipping. And hitting an indi-vidual target – however large it might be – was a different matter entirely.

Unlike the rocket-armed fighters flying regular Defence of the Reich missions, which were equipped with a special control panel for firing their missiles, we would have to make do with the red push-button below the instrument panel that was nor-mally used to jettison our belly tanks (and which the electricians were even now busily rewiring). As the spin-stabilized rockets had a tendency to drift to the right in flight, the actual firing in-structions we were given were a model of brevity: 'At a range of 1,000 metres, aim off eighty metres to the left!'

This was all very well as far as it went, but how to gauge that apparently all-important 1,000 metres? We had no special aim-ing aids, of course, just our standard Revi 16B reflector gun-sight, which projected an illuminated ring in front of the pilot's eyes. The diameter of this ring represented one-tenth of the dis-tance he was from his target. Say, for example, he was attacking a fighter with an average ten-metre wingspan; when the wings of the enemy machine exactly filled the diameter of his sight, he knew he was 100 metres away from it.

It was thus theoretically possible to use the Revi to establish how far away we were from any ship we were attacking... if only someone had deigned to tell us the lengths of the damned tubs we were likely to encounter off the beaches! But unfortunately such trivial bits of information were not imparted to us during the pre-op briefing. In the time remaining I therefore tried to formulate a rough rule of thumb by estimating the likely lengths of various allied vessels. I reckoned that a Liberty or Victory-class merchantman would be about 100 metres long. So if I attacked from the side and the target was filling the width of my gunsight, that would automatically mean that I was the required 1,000 metres away.

All I had to do then was aim off about three-quarters of the ship's length to the left, and I would have complied with the firing instructions to the letter. There was, however, just one other prerequisite to a successful attack: the enemy fighter umbrella over the beachhead would have to turn a blind eye long enough to allow me to carry it out.

At around 09.30hrs we took off. We were flying in three Schwarms – twelve aircraft; twenty-four rockets in all. Major Hohagen was not taking part in this mission. Leading the formation in his stead was Hauptmann Josef Wurmheller, the Staffelkapitän of 9./JG 2. Like Kommodore Oberstleutnant Bühligen, 'Sepp' Wurmheller was another highly experienced and long-serving member of the Geschwader. His personal score was also standing just short of 100 at this time, and he too was wearing the Oak Leaves.

With a rocket under each wing, we were unable to carry our usual belly tanks. But these were not required. The Focke-Wulf's radius of action was some 900 kilometres and the flight to the target area and back was only about half that distance. Our objective was the landing beach to the northeast of Bayeux (which, I later learned, was the one code-named Gold; the westernmost

135

of the three British invasion sectors). The sky was seven-tenths cloud. These were ideal conditions for our purpose. The large gaggles of allied fighters – Spitfires, Mustangs, Thunderbolts and the like, which could be seen patrolling the clear patches of sky – were unlikely to get the drop on our small formation as we flitted in and out of the concealing banks of cumulus.

After about half an hour we crossed Bayeux, where I could see fires already raging. In an effort to deceive the enemy we continued flying out over the Bay of the Seine for several more minutes, planning to mount our attack from seaward. From our height of 3,000 metres I had a panoramic view of the entire invasion area, stretching from the mouth of the River Orne and Caen to the east, to the Cotentin Peninsula in the west. A whole armada of ships, in the truest sense of the word, was spread out below me.

Furthest away from the coast was a line of huge battleships, occasionally belching fire and smoke as they sent another broadside deep inland. Next came the destroyers, troop transports and landing ships, protected by numerous dark-hued barrage balloons. Closest to the shore were the smaller landing craft and countless amphibious vehicles, the majority trailing vivid white wakes as they headed directly for the beaches. As I had not experienced any of the previous allied landings in the Mediterranean, I had no way of judging the scope of this latest enemy undertaking. So although not *totally* overawed by the spectacle, the sheer size of it raised the first serious doubts in my mind. Would we really be able to repel such a powerful force?

Undisturbed either by fighters or naval flak, we completed our run out over the bay and turned through 180 degrees to head back towards the largest concentration of troopships. Because of the allied fighter umbrella over the beachhead area, we wouldn't have the time or the opportunity to position ourselves for a beam attack. It would have to be a high-speed dash straight

136

for the shore – the same direction, of course, in which most of the ships were heading – with an attack on the vessels from directly astern as we flashed past low overhead. But as we approached I saw that the ship almost directly in front of me was, in fact, lying in the water practically broadside on to my line of flight. With mounting excitement I laid off three-quarters of the ship's length to the left and prepared to launch my rockets.

It was only as I got closer, and the target grew bigger, that I realized from the tiny feather of white water that I could see under the ship's stern that it wasn't lying stopped at all, but in fact was moving slowly to the left, and not only that, it was also turning. I quickly reduced speed in order not to overshoot the specified 1,000-metre firing distance and curved fractionally to the left myself, realigning my aim a good full ship's length ahead of the vessel. When I estimated it was large enough to occupy the ring of my gunsight (had I been aiming straight at it), I pressed the red button.

For a second I was enveloped in a brilliant ball of flame and the noise of a thousand howling devils assailed my ears. Never having fired a rocket before in my life, it gave me one hell of a fright. I don't know what I was expecting, but certainly nothing as terrifying as this. The other pilots were also loosing off their rockets and for a moment it was as if the sky around me was filled with fiery comets. Although the missiles produced no recoil when fired, my aircraft bucked slightly as it was relieved of their combined weight.

I quickly rammed the nose down again and hared for the shore. As I crossed the beach at a height of 300 metres, I let fly at the mass of men and matériel packed below. After the spectacular and noisy fireworks that had accompanied the launch of the two rockets, the thumping of my cannon, drowned out by the roar of the engine, sounded like the harmless popping of a cap pistol.

With allied fighters now obviously aware of our presence, it was not advisable to remain over the beachhead area for long. It seemed as if Göring's plans to send in the 'entire Luftwaffe' had yet to materialize, for apart from the twelve of us there wasn't a single German aircraft to be seen in the sky. Under the circumstances we had to abandon all ideas of a co-ordinated low-level attack. It was high time to get upstairs and start playing hide-and-seek in the clouds again if we wanted to make it back to base in one piece. But we weren't returning to Creil. We had been ordered instead to head for Senlis, a town some ten kilometres further to the southeast, where the local racecourse had been earmarked as our new landing ground. We touched down there shortly before 11.00hrs.

After making my way from the racetrack to the small chateau close by that was to serve as both our ops room and our quarters, I was surprised to be congratulated by the Gruppenkommandeur. Apparently Leutnant Walterscheid had witnessed my attack on the ship, which he had identified as a Victory-class transport. His report confirmed that one of my rockets had hit the vessel's stern and exploded, and that the other had gone into the water just behind it.

Major Hohagen couldn't say how many points this would bring me, for, as far as he was aware, the Gruppe had never put in any claims for damage to shipping before. But he was fairly sure that it would be worth the Iron Cross, First Class, at least – especially as I had already been notified that I was to be awarded Iron Cross, Second Class. The latter, incidentally, I would find waiting for me when I returned home from captivity after the war. Of the former there was no sign – perhaps the relevant paperwork had gone astray in the growing chaos and confusion that followed the Normandy landings.

In the meantime our dozen machines had been fully refuelled, re-armed and hidden away under the trees bordering the racetrack. According to the Reichsmarschall's order of the day, we should already be climbing back into them and taking off on our next mission. But as had become all too apparent during our recent anti-shipping sortie, there was clearly some delay to the promised massive counter strike by the Luftwaffe.

Our two Staffeln at Senlis were not even held at readiness. In fact, we were given permission to leave the base. Four of us decided to visit the local municipal swimming pool. And so, incredibly, I spent the afternoon of D-Day sunning myself by the poolside in Senlis, while a lone P-51 circled lazily some 2,000 metres overhead. I presume that it was a reconnaissance machine. But he must have failed to spot our well-camouflaged fighters, for the field was not subjected to any bombing or strafing attacks.

It was not until the evening, when we were all relaxing in the little chateau's main salon, that a call came through from our local Jagdfliegerführer (OC Fighter Forces) at Bernay. It was to inform us that five aircraft of III. Gruppe from Creil would shortly be arriving at Senlis and that three of our number were to join them in an attack on enemy gliders reported to be landing in the Caen area. So there was to be another mission after all, albeit one flown by only a fraction of the Geschwader's available strength.

The five III. Gruppe machines duly touched down at about 19.30hrs. They were led by their Gruppenkommandeur, Hauptmann Herbert Huppertz, who had already shot down three allied fighters during two missions over Caen earlier in the day. The three Senlis pilots who had been selected to accompany them were Leutnant Eichhoff and Fähnrich Beer, both of 2. Staffel, together with myself as the sole representative of 3. Staffel. With each Focke-Wulf carrying a 300-litre auxiliary tank, which would give us an extra hour's flying time, the eight of us took off shortly after 20.00hrs and set course almost due west – 280 degrees – flying at an altitude of 400 metres.

We were well over halfway to our objective when, some ten miles to the northeast of Bernay, we sighted a dozen Mustangs strafing a convoy of German military vehicles heading towards the invasion front. All thoughts of the gliders were abandoned. Our first duty lay in helping our comrades on the ground here and now.

For once the odds were not too bad; only eight to twelve against, and we had the element of surprise on our side. The Americans had probably not seen hide or hair of a Luftwaffe aircraft all day long and were perhaps growing careless. Either that, or they were so intent on attacking the troops below that they failed entirely to notice us as we dropped our belly tanks and crept up into position above and behind them.

At 1,200 metres a light evening mist was already beginning to gather, but from this height we could clearly see the Mustangs as they lined up in turn to make their strafing runs. They were spaced so regularly apart that each of us was able to pick his particular victim before we dived down at them. Mine was just preparing to launch another attack on a section of the convoy that was crossing the bridge over the River Risle. I closed in on him rapidly, but couldn't get within firing range before he had completed his pass.

When he pulled sharply up to the left at the end of his run, however, I was sitting snugly on his tail. His steep turn to port forced me to apply so much deflection that he disappeared momentarily behind my engine cowling. Although I didn't actually see my shots strike home, I knew instinctively that I had hit him. Using the excess of speed built up in my dive, I quickly overhauled him, flying close past his left side to observe the effects of my fire.

It had been absolutely devastating. My burst had caught the enemy fighter squarely in the middle of the fuselage above the wing trailing edge. The high-explosive shells in my ammunition mix had punched large holes in the Mustang's metal skin, the edges of which were glowing a deep red. With the pilot slumped lifeless in his seat, the burning P-51 went down in a shallow dive towards the river. It exploded against the base of a tree on the left bank of the Risle. The trunk immediately burst into flames and within seconds the whole tree was blazing from top to bottom like a giant candle.

We turned back for home, jubilant at having accounted for eight of the enemy without loss to ourselves. Taken in isolation, it was a splendid result. And even when only three of our eight claims were subsequently confirmed, the fact alone that we had returned without casualties on this historic day was achievement enough in itself. But from an overall point of view, our personal successes – whether eight or three – were again just a drop in the ocean.

Eichhoff, Beer and I were nonetheless still buoyed up when we touched down back at Senlis. It was now about 21.30hrs and dusk had fallen. A short while earlier, quite by chance, a couple of war reporters had turned up at the field with their recording van. They were trying to cobble together an up-to-the-minute report from the invasion front. Upon being informed that we were just returning from a combat mission, they rushed over to interview us, thrusting a microphone in front of our faces and demanding to know all about the fight we had been in less than half an hour earlier – you can't get much more recent than that. When our ordeal was over, the three of us were each presented with a copy of the recording they had made. Unfortunately, my disc was lost along with a lot of my other effects after I was shot down the following morning.

That morning – 7 June – began shortly after 05.30hrs when another twelve of the Gruppe's Fw 190s, each carrying two underwing rockets, lifted off from Senlis. The objective was once again the invasion shipping off Gold beach, which might explain why Major Hohagen, who was leading today's mission, had selected me to fly as his wingman. At yesterday's debriefing I had been asked to describe in some detail the rudimentary procedure I had adopted for aiming and launching my rockets. As I was the only pilot to achieve a hit, perhaps he now looked upon me as the unit's anti-shipping expert. Maybe he thought it could do no harm to have me on his wing – even though, in all honesty, I had pointed out that I was also the only pilot lucky enough to have been presented with a target almost sideways on.

We employed similar tactics to the day before, approaching Gold from the seaward side at an altitude of about 1,000 metres and with our throttles wide open. But the situation, both on the water below and in the air all around us, was far less favourable than it had been the day before. The British were on the alert and we stood absolutely no chance of manoeuvring into position for a coordinated rocket attack. We simply had to fire our missiles in the general direction of the ships standing off the beach, trusting more to luck than judgement. Needless to say, we didn't score a single hit.

But I must admit I was surprised when our leader made no move to take us down for a strafing run with our cannon. I could only assume that today's mission included further targets that only the Kommandeur had been briefed on, and which we wingmen, for some reason, had not been told about. So it was a case of sticking close and following his lead.

But then, some 1,500 metres almost directly ahead of me on the sea below, I spotted a large landing ship. It must have been a good 2,000 tons and appeared to be lying stationary in the water, with troops preparing to disembark into a clutch of small amphibious craft hovering alongside. On a sudden impulse – and against every rule of formation-keeping discipline that had ever been drummed into me – I pushed the stick forward, intending to give the vessel a good burst, almost in passing, as it were. I knew that when we got back to base I could expect the mother and father of all roastings for leaving my number one – the Kommandeur himself, no less – alone and unprotected for those few moments. But I would be back in my place on his wing in next to no time, I thought to myself... except that things didn't quite turn out that way.

As I dived at the ship I opened up with everything I had. Fire from my four 20-mm cannon and two heavy machine guns raked the vessel's deck. At first there was no return fire from my selected target, but the gun crews on all the surrounding ships seemed suddenly to wake up to the fact that one of their number was under attack from the air. Tracer came at me from all sides. I felt as if I was flying into a glowing spider's web.

I was almost directly above the landing ship, and just about to pull up out of danger, when I felt the fuselage of my machine take several hits. Then the engine caught a packet. It immediately started to spray oil all over the windscreen and I realized that I had finally pushed my luck too far. This was it – no choices this time. I had to bale out.

But I needed to gain some height before I could safely take to my parachute. I pulled the nose of the Focke-Wulf up into a steep climb. With the engine already beginning to labour, I was losing speed rapidly and still taking hits from the ships that continued to fire at me furiously. At 600 metres I decided it was time to go. I had already completed the preparatory bale-out ritual – everything unbuckled and undone – but this time I decided to be more careful. I wasn't going to roll out over the side of the cockpit and risk getting trapped again. I would catapult myself out cleanly.

Lifting myself from my seat, I gave the stick a hefty kick with my right foot. As expected, the machine instantly tipped forward on to its nose and I was shot quite comfortably straight out of the cockpit by the sudden force of the negative g. But then the slipstream caught me and hurled me backwards against the tailplane.

Fortunately, I hit it with my left shoulder. I say fortunately because it could so easily have been my head or right shoulder that took the blow, which would have meant 'curtains' on the spot or not being able to use my right hand to open my parachute. As it was, I hardly felt a thing. It was only later in hospital that I was told I had broken not only my shoulder blade, but my collar-bone, upper arm and three ribs as well.

I must have been in a state of some shock, however, for as I drifted slowly down in my parachute everything around me seemed to be cocooned in an eerie silence. The light flak now coming up at me from the ship I had just attacked, the bullets singing past my ears and tearing a few small holes in the silk canopy of my 'chute – none of it really registered. A stiff breeze was driving me towards the beach at Ver-sur-Mer. And it wasn't until I was just a few metres off the ground that people finally stopped using me for target practice.

In those days there was about a 100-metre wide stretch of sand and sea-grass between the water's edge and the rising land on which the village stood. And it was in the middle of this that I came gently to earth, and it was only when I touched the ground that my hearing slowly started to return and I began to feel the pain in my left shoulder.

CHAPTER 8

CAPTIVITY

The first thing to do was to get out of my parachute, which was developing a mind of its own and starting to drag me through the spiky grass. I managed this with my one good arm and then tried to conceal both it and myself in what little cover there was on the exposed beach. In my innocence – ignorance, if you like – I imagined that if only I could keep out of sight long enough, we would launch the promised counter-attack, drive the Tommys back into the water, and take the opportunity to rescue me at the same time.

But, instead of this wishful scenario, it wasn't long before I saw through the grass two upturned soup bowls slowly approaching me – British helmets! Their wearers were advancing with extreme caution, prodding the sand ahead of them with thin sticks as they came. When they were about twenty metres away from me they raised their rifles and shouted: "Hands up!" In those days my English was non-existent, but their meaning was obvious. I still had my pride as a Luftwaffe officer, however, and didn't want to subject myself to this indignity. So instead, and with some justification, I remained lying on the ground, my face screwed up in pain, and waved at them with my right arm.

They cottoned on at once. When they got to me they helped me to my feet; but not before first confiscating my silk parachute. Then they searched me for weapons. But in the west none of us wore side arms when flying on operations. Finally, they indicated that I was to accompany them. We were to walk in single file, with me in the middle, while they resumed their ceremonial prodding of the ground, explaining that we were in the middle of a German minefield.

"Bugger it," I thought to myself, "after all that, and now you're probably going to die a hero's death blown up by one of our own mines." But we got out safely and made our way to a small tent with a red cross painted on it. Here a medic gave me first aid by folding my left forearm against the upper arm and binding both tightly together with my shoulder. It made the pain much more bearable.

I must say those lads treated me very well. They got me a warm blanket – it was still rather chilly this early in the morning – and motioned for me to sit or lie down next to the tent. They gave me a mug of hot cocoa and offered me a cigarette, which I gratefully accepted. It must have been my nerves, for up until that time I had been a strict non-smoker. (I was to remain a slave to the weed from that 7 June 1944 until finally giving up the habit in 1962.)

As I lay there sipping my cocoa and smoking, I was able to watch the vast amounts of war matériel pouring ashore over the kilometre-long stretch of beach in front of me. Marshals were herding every vehicle on to some sort of artificial track that led from the beach up to the high ground immediately next to Ver-sur-Mer – and all this was going on without the slightest sign of any countermeasures from our side. The Tommys must have pushed quite a way inland already. Only once did a mine go up between the landing craft crowding the water's edge, but it did no damage as far as I could tell.

CAPTIVITY

In the afternoon I was taken to a small patch of open ground in the centre of Ver-sur-Mer, which was being used as a collecting point for the first German prisoners. About twenty were already there. I hadn't seen a single local inhabitant as I walked through the ruined village, which had been badly knocked about by the pre-invasion bombardment. Two armed sentries were patrolling the low stone wall that enclosed the area of grass, no more than about thirty metres square, that we now occupied. A few tents had already been put up to offer us some protection from the cold of the night ahead. From this I deduced that our captors were not yet prepared, or able, to transport us back to England.

From our 'prison camp' in the village I could no longer see the beach itself, but the battleships lying further out to sea were still clearly visible. After darkness had fallen they provided an awe-inspiring and fascinating spectacle. Every few minutes one or other of them would fire a salvo from its enormous 40-cm guns. For a moment a vivid orange cloud would blossom out of the blackness and from it would emerge the glowing pinpricks of the shells as they climbed slowly – or so it appeared from this distance – high into the sky on their way inland... and still no evidence whatsoever of any counterattack, either by land, sea or air.

This, together with the fact that I had been separated from my comrades, the Staffel and the Geschwader, and was no longer able to help Germany in her present hour of need, filled me with a sense of deep depression. Naturally, my thoughts turned to my family back in Rosenheim, especially my mother and sister, whose letters to me would now be returned to them stamped 'Fallen for Greater Germany'. But fortunately it was only a few weeks before they learned from information broadcast by the British authorities that I had survived and was in captivity only slightly wounded.

The author on home leave in 1943 pictured with his
grandmother ...

My grandmother, strange to relate, had not needed official
confirmation. She was a keen amateur astrologist. And although
we often poked fun at her for her belief in the stars, she had
lost no time in drawing up a chart of the constellations for 7
June, the day I had gone missing. This, she insisted, showed
beyond a shadow of a doubt that I was very much alive. Just
how right she was may be judged from the fact that both the
chart and I are still in existence to this day.

Thoughts of escape also crossed my mind. It would not have
been difficult. But I knew that I wouldn't get far with my useless
left arm. Instead I spent a sleepless night worrying about what
the future held in store. I must have finally dozed off, for I was
suddenly woken again at about 6am by the angry hammering
of flak out to sea. Then I heard the roar of fighter engines, un-

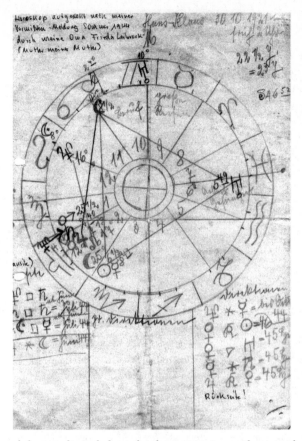

... and the astrological chart she drew up to 'prove' her grandson
was still alive despite being reported missing.

mistakably Fw 190s, somewhere close by. Could it have been
the Geschwader – perhaps even my own Staffel – attacking the
shipping off Gold for the third morning in a row? But after that
– nothing. For the remainder of the day the only sounds of battle were the distant rumbles of naval gunfire as the enemy's
heavy warships kept up their bombardment of our ground

149

forces now fighting far inland.

After night fell on this 8 June we were taken down to the beach together with groups of other prisoners and put aboard a landing craft for the trip across the Channel. When we landed in England the wounded were separated from the rest and taken by train to a military hospital in Preston, Lancashire. It was here that I was operated upon; that is, the broken bones were put back into place and an adhesive dressing was applied to my left arm and shoulder.

The treatment and medical attention that I received was excellent, although the chloroform that was the standard anaesthetic in those days meant that one came to again after the operation feeling perfectly lousy. It affected different people in different ways. While still dozy and not yet fully conscious, the grizzled old soldier in the bed next to mine kept yelling over and over again at the top of his voice, "Chérie, you absolutely stink of Calvados!" – so clearly his time in Normandy hadn't been entirely wasted.

The one thing I couldn't stand was the English idea of breakfast consisting of tea with milk, and porridge served with pappy white bread; especially as I had always loathed porridge, even as a boy. But all in all our captors stuck to the rules of the Geneva Convention, and there was nothing really to complain about. The day after my operation I was allowed out for a walk in the hospital grounds with a few of the other prisoners.

A wire fence divided us from the parade ground of the neighbouring barracks. Naturally curious to see how things were done 'on the other side' we strolled across. We were deeply impressed by the British drill sergeant – bullet-headed, chiselled chin you could sharpen a flint on – who was screaming orders at a bunch of obviously raw recruits in a voice that would have made any German kapo green with envy. Of course, he knew full well who was watching him through the wire and was probably laying it on a bit thick just for our benefit.

After about a fortnight an elderly captain, jovial and more than a little portly, came to collect me. He seemed quite friendly and so I asked him, more by gestures than in words, where we were going. He murmured something or other in reply and I caught a word that sounded like 'sanatorium', but I didn't believe this for a moment. Although of German stock himself, I'm sure that His Majesty King George VI's hospitality didn't extend as far as convalescent leave for prisoners of war.

But I *had* heard somewhere that the English had a camp something along the lines of the Luftwaffe's own reception and interrogation centre for shot-down allied flyers at Oberursel, in the Taunus hills outside Frankfurt. I could therefore make a fairly good guess as to where we were actually heading. While waiting for the train at Preston station the captain treated me to a coffee, which we drank standing at the buffet counter. The other passengers were watching me with patently mixed feelings, although none was openly hostile.

I was given to understand that our rail journey was to last about four hours and would take us somewhere to the west of London. After two hours or so the captain unpacked a couple of ham and lettuce sandwiches, one of which he gave to me. Thus fortified, he started to nod off. But he kept jerking into wakefulness again, eyeing me somewhat distrustfully each time he did so. I had made myself comfortable in a window seat and was gazing with interest at the passing landscape, while he, for obvious reasons, sat diagonally across from me next to the door leading out into the corridor.

Finally, his tiredness got the better of him. "Dammit, let's get some sleep", he grunted, forsaking all military and patriotic responsibilities in favour of a quick nap. I dutifully closed my eyes until he had dropped off. I had given up all thoughts of an escape attempt from the speeding train anyway.

He awoke as the carriage rattled over the points outside one
of London's main railway stations, and was clearly relieved to
see me still sitting obediently in my corner by the window. It
was another two hours before he was finally able to deliver me
to the 'convalescent home'. First I was formally and rather
brusquely assigned a room, and then had to change out of my
flying overalls into a set of British battledress tunic and trousers
that had been dyed black and had the letters POW – for prisoner-of-war – painted across the back.

The following morning my interrogation began. It was conducted by a British colonel, who introduced himself to me as
Oberst 'King' (although I subsequently discovered that this was
not his real name). He spoke flawless German. According to
the rules, all I was obliged to tell him was my rank, name and
home address – plus, at most, any inconsequential personal details I might care to impart.

At first he stuck to this format, no doubt in an attempt to
gain my confidence and get me to reveal things that could be
of interest to him. When I mentioned to him that I played the
cello, he feigned astonishment, saying that from my appearance
(at that time I had a full head of dark hair and a brown sun-
tanned face) he had me pegged more for a gypsy than a typical
German – let alone an officer in the armed forces. It was then
my turn to be astonished. How could a man in his position sub-
scribe to such views? Did he really believe in that sort of racial
propaganda, or was this just another of his ploys to make me
start talking?

At my next interrogation, for which I was woken in the middle of the night, he came straight to the point. First of all he
wanted to know which airfield I had taken off from on my last
flight, to which unit I belonged, and how many operational aircraft we had. When I refused categorically to answer these
questions, he tried threatening me, because for one, I was not

carrying my 'Frontflugausweis' – my front-line flying pass, which admittedly I had forgotten to put in my pocket – but was simply wearing an identity tag that could quite easily be false, and another, there were no badges of rank on my flying overalls (these latter were newly issued and I had not yet had the time to sew my Leutnant's wing and bar insignia on the sleeves).

In the light of the above, he warned me, he was fully entitled to classify me as 'illegal' – in other words, as a partisan – which gave him the right to have me put up against a wall and shot. This sounded decidedly unhealthy. But my continued refusal to answer had little to do with any great display of courage on my part. Based on the given facts, his hypothesis was simply too ridiculous. Just how did he suppose I engaged in partisan activity while flying on operations? Besides, he didn't seem to be taking the matter too seriously himself. He soon let it drop, for in the meantime he had found other ways of gathering information about me.

On the fourth day of my questioning he placed a copy of the weekly magazine *Berliner Illustrierte Zeitung* in front of me. It was the issue dated 20 April 1944 (coincidentally the Führer's birthday) containing a double-spread illustrated feature on an unidentified 'Jagdgeschwader in the West'. He had folded the paper so that all I could see of it was a picture of my Gruppenkommandeur, Major Hohagen. Oberst King told me that I need say no more. He now knew all there was to be known about me. I was a member of 3. Staffel of the 'renowned' Jagdgeschwader Richthofen. I had been with the unit since March 1944, and this was a picture of my commanding officer. He also identified the airfield I had taken off from; namely Cormeilles.

This last snippet gave me a great deal of satisfaction, for we had vacated Cormeilles some three weeks before my last mission. So the information provided to the British by the French resistance, or perhaps even by French workers employed by our own supply services, was at least that long out of date, if not more. Our recent frequent moves from one landing ground to another suddenly began to make more sense.

Having thus established my background in his own mind, Oberst King went off on another tack. He now wanted to know something about our tactics in the air. He tried to provoke some sort of reaction out of me by implying that we German fighter pilots were not all that skilled and weren't achieving very much. I'm afraid I rose to the bait by describing the encounters we had had on 25 May and the evening of 6 June, both of which had ended very much in our favour. I could tell from the expression on his face that he thought I was shooting a line. But after rooting around in some files he seemed to have a change of mind, and this subject too was quietly shelved.

Then, of course, there came the question of what exactly had I been fighting for and why was I prepared to lay down my life for Hitler. Here I was on safer ground. I explained that, as a boy growing up in the Germany of the 'twenties and 'thirties, I could not help but be influenced by the mood of the times; the desire to right the wrongs of the hated Versailles Treaty and to see Germany emerge as an equal among her European neighbours as set out in the constitution of the Weimar Republic. These were the principles for which I was willing to lay down my life – not for the person of Hitler.

I warmed to my subject, describing the historical developments in Germany prior to World War One and even going back as far as the events of 1848. This resulted in my being visited the following day by another German-speaking officer. He was carrying a thick book under his arm. This was an historical tome, written in German, which he presented to me as reading material for the rest of my stay. In the course of a long stroll through the extensive grounds surrounding the camp, he encouraged me to expound further on the causes and reasons for Hitler's rise to power. I noticed that he voiced no opinions of his own during our discussion and assumed – as the war was still on – that the Geneva Convention prohibited him from influencing me politically in any way.

I never did get to read his book, however, for on the very next day, after about a week of my sojourn, I was taken along with several others to a camp near Derby in central England. This turned out to be a transit camp where we joined some fifty other German officers who were undergoing medical examination before transfer elsewhere. And the fact that we had to parade in front of an American general left us in little doubt where that was to be. We were in for a trip across the big pond to a prisoner-of-war camp in the United States.

After just two days at Derby we left for Liverpool, where we were put aboard a large troop transport. Our accommodation was somewhat unusual. We didn't particularly mind being herded together ten or twenty to a cabin, but the fact that the doors were reinforced by steel grilles and laced with barbed wire, with an armed GI standing guard in front of each one, did strike us as a trifle excessive. Apparently – and this I only discovered later – it was honestly believed that we Germans were capable of the most dastardly acts. Many feared, for example, that we might somehow overpower the ship's crew and sail it ourselves to a German-held port!

In complete contrast to life in our cabins below, when we were escorted up to the officers' mess for dinner on the first evening we were welcomed as 'guests of the US Navy' by the captain, who also wished us *bon appetit* before we sat down to eat. I must admit to finding the whole situation somehow schizophrenic, but there was nonetheless a definite undercurrent of mutual respect between the two sides on board the ship. At around noon each day we were allowed up on deck for about half an hour to get a breath of fresh air. As an absolute land-lubber, it was my first taste of the delights to be had from an ocean cruise – even if it was one being undertaken in rather exceptional circumstances.

We discovered that our ship was just one of a large convoy. All around us other freighters and transports were butting their way through the enormous waves (enormous to someone like me, that is, who was more accustomed to the ripples on a Bavarian lake). The vessels were spaced so far apart, and over such a wide area of ocean, that the outer edges of the convoy could not be seen. Now and again we would catch a glimpse of the sleek form of a destroyer out on the horizon, one of the flotilla of escort vessels that were chivvying us along like so many sheepdogs guarding their precious flock.

On a couple of occasions during the crossing the U-boat alarm was actually sounded. We then had to muster on deck wearing our life jackets. As may be imagined, our feelings were decidedly mixed. While wishing our U-boat boys every success, our sense of patriotism did not stretch quite so far as to relish the idea of being sent to the bottom ourselves.

After a good week at sea we were ordered up on deck again, but this time we were instructed to take all our personal belongings with us. It was around noon on 12 July 1944, as I can remember quite vividly, and in a few hours' time we would be docking in New York harbour, where we were to be immediately transferred on to a train that would be waiting to take us on the next stage of our journey. The famous skyline of Manhattan – that symbol of 'capitalist decadence' as we had been brought up to believe – was already beginning to loom up over the horizon.

As we slowly made our way up the East River in the shadow of the huge skyscrapers, a '150 per center' among our ranks suggested that we all deliberately turn our backs and look in the other direction in order to display our complete indifference and not to give the Amis – as we referred to the Americans – the satisfaction of witnessing our sense of wonder and admiration.

Speaking personally, my feelings weren't those of wonder and admiration. Confronted by this solid mass of architecture towering into the sky, the mighty assemblage of shipping in the river, the endless expanse of docks and wharves with their forests of cranes, what I felt could be more accurately described as total disbelief and shock. As a European I simply couldn't take in the vast scale of everything I was seeing.

The transfer from ship to train, the latter also unlike anything I had ever experienced in Germany or France, went without a hitch. It wasn't long before we were all securely inside the compartments to which we had been assigned. An armed GI again stood guard at either end of the carriage to make sure that we didn't leave our seats. The only time we were permitted to do so was when we had to go to the toilet. This involved a ritual that reminded me strongly of my first year at school: finger held up in the air to attract the teacher's – sorry, the guard's – attention, await his affirmative nod, and then straight to the toilet and back with no talking.

Whenever we stopped at a station the windows would have to be closed and the blinds pulled down – and again no talking. You couldn't be too careful. After all, these 'damned Krauts' might have been hatching a plot to jump out of the windows and take the local townspeople hostage; maybe even force the train driver to head for the Mexican border (even if Mexico *had* declared war on Germany more than two years earlier). In fact, all the signs were that the train actually was heading southwards.

On the second day of the journey we stopped, if I remember rightly, at Nashville, Tennessee, a name that didn't mean anything to me at that time. As on the day before, we were escorted under guard into the station restaurant, where we were allowed to seat ourselves at the neatly laid tables. After a little while two black waitresses poked their heads round the kitchen door and stared at us, their eyes wide with fright. When they saw that several armed GIs were standing guard over us, they ventured hesitantly into the room and started to serve us.

Their curiosity soon got the better of their fear and before long they were inspecting us from head to foot. It all seemed very strange. Eventually, one of our number who spoke English asked them why they had been so frightened of us at first. When he translated their reply we were all dumbstruck. Apparently they had been terrified when told that they were going to have to serve lunch to a crowd of German prisoners-of-war. According to what they had heard, Germans were 'some kind of devils with horns and cloven hooves!' Further comment is superfluous.

That afternoon we passed through Memphis. We were all impressed by the awesome size of the River Mississippi. Was everything bigger in this country? But for me, despite the majesty of its powerful slow-moving current, the mighty Mississippi could not compare with the tumbling crystal waters of the much smaller River Inn of my boyhood. It was not long after leaving Memphis that our train pulled into the provincial township of Como, Mississippi. This was our destination, and from here we were taken by road to our new home, Camp Como, several kilometres out in the country. What little we could see of the landscape on the way was not very encouraging: a flat, almost barren plain baked dry and dusty by the summer sun blazing down out of a milky-white sky.

Knots of prisoners were standing at the camp gates eagerly scanning the faces of us newcomers hoping to spot a friend or acquaintance from earlier shared 'days of glory'. The camp itself consisted of about sixty large wooden barracks huts standing on concrete pillars nearly a metre high (presumably to discourage tunnelling). Each hut was divided into four separate compartments, which shared a long communal veranda running along the front of the building.

This rustic style gave the place something of a homely, almost cosy feel. In the centre of the camp, high above everything else, was a large wooden water tower of the sort familiar from countless Wild West films. Thin rivulets of water trickled constantly from the leaky metal tank atop the wooden structure. When the heat became too unbearable these provided blessed relief to anyone standing beneath them.

At the four corners of the camp, each side of which was about 200 metres long, stood a watchtower. These were equipped with searchlights and manned twenty-four hours a day by armed guards, whose job was to make sure that nobody made a break for it – they, the guards, were not always successful, I might add. Between the towers stretched a double fence, some three metres in height, the top of which was angled inwards and covered in barbed wire. Immediately outside the camp were the living quarters of the guard personnel and a hospital that served both the camp staff and prisoners alike.

After first dumping our things in the huts, we went outside to get to know the establishment's occupants. There were about 200 men already in the camp. They were all ex-Afrika Korps, the vast majority of them taken prisoner after the fall of Tunisia in the spring of 1943. Although they had arrived at Como only a few weeks before us, they had been in allied captivity for well over a year and were thus able to pass on all sorts of handy tips and useful advice.

Further batches of prisoners would continue to arrive over the course of the coming weeks so that, by the end of September, the camp contained its full complement of close on 1,000 men. To my pleasant surprise I bumped into an old friend and comrade from my training days with LKS 4 at Fürstenfeldbruck who, like me, had also gone on to serve with JG 2 in France.

The compartments mentioned above each comprised a kind of anteroom, or lobby, with two bedrooms adjoining. With two prisoners sharing a bedroom, this meant that we lived together in groups of four. The rooms were, on the whole, quite comfortable, although they had looked a bit bleak and forlorn when we first arrived. They had previously been occupied by Italians – also apparently captured in North Africa – who seemed to have set little store on gracious living. The only decorations were a few faded pin-ups still adorning the walls. But after we had added a few personal touches they became much more homely.

With traditional German thoroughness and ingenuity we set about producing picture frames for our family photos, as well as hand-painted lampshades, bookcases and the like. We even hung curtains at the windows and made elaborate nameplates for the front doors. These latter usually reflected the occupants' home towns or states. As I lived with a group hailing mostly from Lower Saxony, our door was decorated with that province's rearing white horse with the name 'Ems', the region's largest river, carved beneath it.

According to military law a so-called 'camp elder' had to be appointed. His task would be to liaise with the American commandant of the camp, a Captain Henkle (of German descent), and ensure that any orders or instructions given were properly carried out. He would, in effect, be responsible for the internal running of the camp and the maintenance of military discipline among the prisoners.

The job fell to the highest-ranking officer among us, an infantry Oberst by the name of Seiderer, who came from Freising, a town not far to the north of Munich. He was, thank the Lord, neither a stickler for the minutiae of military regulations, nor a political 150 per center, but a solid and down-to-earth front-line soldier. He performed his duties fairly and conscientiously and soon won the trust and respect of the Americans. A small advisory staff helped him manage the everyday affairs of the camp and look after our best interests.

Our official duties within the camp were not exactly onerous. We were required to parade in ranks of three at 07.00hrs every morning to be counted, we were expected to mess together at lunch and dinner – and that was about it. After dinner each evening a spokesman for the camp leaders would make one or two administrative announcements. More importantly, he would also read out that day's Wehrmacht communiqué broadcast from Germany. This was received via a long-wave radio that one of the signals officers had been able to put together from components he had gathered from somewhere or other. It was a precious link with home that was kept successfully hidden from the Amis until the end of the war.

With little of an official nature to keep us occupied, we turned our attention to our surroundings. The Italians had been just as neglectful of the camp's open spaces as they had been of their living quarters. When we arrived the huts stood on a barren and dusty expanse of ground broken only here and there by a few tufts of coarse grass. We were determined to improve this depressing vista. We had the necessary money; for in accordance with the rules of the Hague Convention, prisoners-of-war of commissioned rank were entitled to receive pay to allow them to buy personal items from the camp canteen (we were even permitted to purchase one bottle of beer per day).

As a Leutnant I got the equivalent of forty US dollars a month in camp currency. Higher ranks received correspondingly more. Every one of us contributed a percentage of his money to a central fund and a considerable sum quickly accrued. This was then paid over to the camp authorities, who arranged for the supply of small garden tools, grass and flower seeds, and suchlike. Full of enthusiasm, we were soon hard at work. Alongside the steps up to the verandas and around the verandas themselves we planted fast-growing climbers. Water was in plentiful supply and so, with the heat of the sun, it was not long before green shoots started to appear all over the camp and the first creepers began climbing up the posts and railings outside the huts.

But the most important task, which every prisoner had to confront and tackle on his own, was to find something that would occupy his mind and keep the dreaded 'camp twitches' at bay. We were particularly fortunate in the unusually high level of education and learning among the 1,000 or so officers at Como. In addition to the regular soldiers, many had been academics in civilian life, which offered possibilities for a wide range of activities.

Among us there were college professors and schoolteachers versed in all kinds of subjects: mathematics, physics, languages, philosophy and astronomy. We had sports instructors, artists and professional musicians, including an orchestral conductor. From the world of theatre there was a director, several actors and a make-up man (the last was to play an important part, not only in our drama productions, but also in our future escape plans).

With such a wealth of talent to hand, it was decided to organize the camp along the lines of a university. There would be two terms in the year: the summer term devoted to sports, and the winter term to studies. Our academics were more than happy to offer their services as lecturers and teachers, for this was also an ideal way for them to break up the monotony of life in the camp.

As it was by now August and the 'summer term' was already

upon us, sports equipment was ordered (again to be paid for from the common fund) and work was started on the necessary facilities. Two tennis courts were laid out – minus the high wire fencing, of course – and covered with a surface layer of fine red ash. We also made a 400-metre running track, dug a long-jump pit, and constructed horizontal and parallel bars for the gymnasts.

To help in the levelling of the cinder running track, the camp authorities kindly made available an ancient cast-iron roller. It took the strength of four men to move this museum piece, which, it was said, dated back to the War of Independence, when its motive power was provided by negro slaves.

It still gives me a certain pang of guilt, even after all these years, to have to admit that we marked out the white lines of the tennis courts with fine white flour! At a time when our nearest and dearest at home were under strict rationing and having to tighten their belts, this could only be described as criminal waste. But we had been supplied with an abundance of flour and were simply observing that old soldiers' dictum: never return unused rations to stores – you'll only be issued with less next time.

Our cultural needs were also well catered for. The theatre director had gathered together a talented group of players. With the assistance of the make-up artist they even ventured to stage Gotthold Lessing's 18th-century comedy 'Minna von Barnhelm', with the unmistakably masculine Minna receiving by far the loudest round of applause. The undisputed success of the season, however, was 'The Green Light', a thriller with no female roles, which was specially written by an Oberleutnant in the camp who had been a lawyer in Vienna in civilian life.

But our main cultural fare was music. A symphony orchestra of almost professional standards was assembled under the leadership of our conductor. The larger instruments such as the piano, double-bass, drums and brass were again acquired through the camp's central funds, while the smaller violins, violas, cellos and woodwind instruments were purchased individually by those able to play them. For example, I clubbed together with a comrade to pay sixty dollars for a cello, which we then took turns to play. Several classical string quartets, sometimes enlarged to quintets, were also formed from among the members of the orchestra. One of these I enriched with my own modest musical talents.

The orchestra gave one concert a month, always on a Sunday. The performances were invariably very well received as our quality of playing, even if I do say so myself, was not at all bad. Our repertoire included such pieces as Beethoven's Fifth Piano Concerto, the Alpine Symphony by Richard Strauss and, of course, Dvořák's New World Symphony. A number of the American officers on the camp staff made a point of attending our concerts whenever their duties permitted, and this latter item always went down well with them.

Our string quartet also tackled one or two more difficult compositions, among them Schubert's Death and the Maiden. This required a certain amount of expertise and a whole lot of practice. But time to practise was one thing we were not short of at Como.

Theatrical and musical activities were not restricted to either the summer or winter term, but went on all year round. There was one comical incident when the camp announcer made a Freudian slip. He was reading out various items of information to do with our everyday life in camp and had just come to the end of a long litany of announcements, including the names of those who had mail to collect, when he turned to the subject of the following Sunday's orchestral programme. He had simply jotted down '5th Symphony by L. Beethoven' on his piece of paper, but – with the lengthy list of names and ranks he had just ploughed through probably still in his mind – he unthinkingly read it out as: "5th Symphony by *Leutnant* Beethoven". There was such a storm of laughter in the room that the walls shook and a couple of guards came rushing in with weapons drawn thinking that they had a riot on their hands.

During the winter term of 1944/45 I decided it was high time that I started to learn English, and so put my name down for an interpreter's course. I successfully managed to complete it, thereby qualifying as an assistant interpreter. The details of everybody who enrolled in, and passed, any of the many and varied courses on offer to us were documented in special prisoner-of-war certificate books, and all qualifications thus gained and attested to were officially recognized by the German authorities after our return to the homeland.

For as long as the war lasted we were very well off in material terms. Each side was conscious of its own prisoners in enemy hands, and so the rules of the Geneva Convention were strictly observed. Among other things, this meant that we were entitled to the same level of rations and medical care as American troops in the Zone of the Interior. After a few initial difficulties the mail system also got into its stride and we regularly began to receive (via neutral Switzerland) letters and parcels from our families at home. All correspondence was, of course, subject to censorship, as became apparent from the occasional offending passage in our letters that had been carefully blacked out.

Such minor irritations aside, we really had little to complain about. The absolute fairness with which we were treated by our captors – and the truly international nature of the world of science – was demonstrated by an incident involving our professor of astronomy. Apparently, in 1945 a comet was expected to enter our solar system. Not knowing what havoc it might cause, it was publicly announced in the press that a prize would be awarded to the person, or persons, who could calculate its likely course. Our astronomer read about this competition in the newspaper and applied to enter. It caused a minor sensation in the camp when he was later declared to be the joint winner together with an American observatory.

Despite all these extra-curricular activities, the fact could not be ignored that we were still, first and foremost, prisoners-of-war – which brings us to the subject of escape attempts. My lack of proper English ruled me out as an escaper, but just to know that they were going on, just to be able to help – in however small a way – filled one with a certain excitement, tension and, above all, a real sense of satisfaction.

None of the successful escapees from Como ever got all the way back to Germany, it must be said. But geography was overwhelmingly in our captors' favour. The only ray of hope was the port of New Orleans, some 600 kilometres away near the mouth of the Mississippi. From here it might just have been possible to get aboard a ship bound for one of the neutral countries of Central or South America. But the odds against this were so high as to be almost non-existent.

To stand even the remotest chance of success an escapee had to have four things: sufficient money, the right clothes, excellent English (spoken with an American accent) and the ability to act and behave like an American. Just one of the camp's 1,000 inmates possessed all four of these attributes. They even got him as far as New Orleans, but there his big mouth let him down. He climbed on a streetcar, not noticing that this was reserved for blacks only. When this was pointed out to him in no uncertain fashion, he reacted violently and a massive free-for-all broke out.

The upshot was that he was returned to us after a four-week absence, still looking somewhat the worse for wear, and promptly sentenced to another four weeks in solitary. This might well have been construed as a contravention of the Hague

Convention. But the Americans had a ready answer. The four weeks were not a punishment. They were a term of quarantine imposed to prevent the possible spread among us POWs of any contagious disease he may have picked up on his travels. A likely story, there had been no mention on the radio or in the press of any epidemic in the area.

Another group of escapees managed to make it to the banks of the Mississippi which, at its nearest point, was only about thirty kilometres away from the camp. Here they assembled a couple of kayaks out of the wooden frames and sheets cut from rubberised waterproof raincoats that they had prepared earlier and carted with them to the river. They set off southwards for the delta, travelling only by night and hiding up during the hours of daylight. They didn't make it very far before being spotted, however, and they too were all brought back to Como to face the music.

Two others pulled off an even more daring escape – one almost worthy of a film – by dressing up as a pair of Ami officers. Wearing their bogus uniforms, some of the items 'organized', other bits skilfully hand-made, they marched boldly out of the front gate shortly after the guards had been changed. Strolling casually over to the motor pool, they purloined a jeep and disappeared in the direction of New Orleans. Attempting perhaps to be too clever, they stopped in a patch of woodland, where they set about trying to disguise the vehicle's military markings. But they were being watched by a ranger, who brought their excursion to an abrupt and inglorious end.

This episode had an unforeseen sequel, for the pair were hauled up in front of a military tribunal. Their temporary 'borrowing' of the jeep was looked upon as auto theft, a crime seemingly comparable to horse stealing in the bad old days of the West. And although they might not end up hanging from the nearest tree, it could mean a lengthy term in jail. Luckily, the judges did not lack a spirit of sportsmanship. They handed down a sentence that ultimately allowed the two to be returned home at about the same time as the rest of us.

Incidentally, we regarded our escape attempts in something of a sporting light too, even if each did require planning with an almost general staff-like precision. It was always good to put one over on the Amis. The first thing that had to be done was to find the necessary amount of 'real' US dollars, our camp currency being useless outside the wire.

This was not all that difficult, as the GIs were very keen on anything hand-made by German POWs. Some of our more gifted comrades did a roaring trade in such things as violins – made either of wood, which could be easily procured, or out of thousands of matchsticks – wooden ornaments or sculptures of all kinds (the female form was always a hot favourite), decorated lampshades and paintings. These items were all paid for in cash, twenty-five per cent of which had to go to the camp committee, who administered it as a secret 'escape fund'.

Any clothing, either civilian or military, that was required for a planned escape attempt would be made by the tailors of the Betriebskompanie, or 'servicing company'. This was modelled along the lines of the Luftwaffe's airfield servicing companies. It was composed of a group of about thirty NCOs and other ranks, all craftsmen or artisans skilled in a wide variety of trades and professions, who looked after the camp's internal maintenance and day-to-day needs. We had our own bakers, for example, who ensured that we were supplied with German-style bread. And on a more clandestine level there were metalworkers who could provide authentic-looking American badges and insignia – at least up to the rank of captain – simply by fashioning them out of empty tin cans.

Once a group of would-be escapees – usually numbering between two and six – had formulated a plan it had to be submitted to the escape committee. If it was given the go-ahead, the requisite funds were allocated and the date, time and exact spot for the attempt would be fixed. Most attempts were made during the hours of darkness, of course, preferably during a new moon period, or half moon at the very most. Once these details were settled, the following arrangements had to be put in place for the actual execution of the breakout:

- Depending upon the direction of the wind on the night, the occupants of the huts nearest to the spot in the wire where the escape was to be made had to bank up their stoves in order to produce as much covering smoke as possible. Time: H-hour minus twenty minutes.

- H-hour minus five minutes: two men had to crawl across to the wire, cut a hole of just under a metre square in both the inner and outer fences, and then remain in place flat on the ground under cover of the wire. (These two would be armed with a pair of wire-cutters that someone had once 'liberated'. They were the camp's prized possession, second perhaps only to the secret radio, and were guarded like the crown jewels.)

- H-hour: the escape group, together with whatever luggage or equipment that needed to be taken, to exit through the wire.

- Immediately thereafter, the 'cutting party' were to repair the hole in the wire and return to their hut.

As far as I am aware, the guards never once caught a group while it was in the act of escaping through the wire. The next and far more difficult problem arose on the morning following the escape when we were paraded to be counted – how to hide the fact that several of our number were missing? We came up with an ingenious solution.

Like every army in the world the Americans had a strict system of drill, which we were able to turn to our advantage. On parade we always had to fall in in three ranks, one behind the other. Our senior officer would then give the command: 'Attention!', and we would stand there like stuffed dummies while he reported the number of POWs present and correct on parade to the American camp commandant. This was checked by the duty sergeant, who strode along the front rank counting off the files and then multiplying their number by three to arrive at the final total.

But all was not as it seemed. Our theatre make-up artist had made six extremely life-like but very different dummy heads (I recall one having an unshaven appearance and another with a large sticking plaster on its cheek). These could be mounted on simple frames, which were then dressed in POW clothing. On the morning after an escape each of the dummies – their exact number determined by how many men had got away – would be carried out on to the parade ground by two 'minders'. This trio was surrounded by a close knot of other prisoners who masked their movements until all three, the two men with the dummy between them, had taken their place in the rear rank.

With the rest of us brought to attention and also standing ramrod straight and stock still, the subterfuge was complete and practically impossible to detect. (In fact, the Amis didn't realize what had been happening until the end of the war, when we finally confessed to what we had been up to – and then even they saw the funny side of it.)

That wasn't quite all, however. We couldn't keep up the pretence forever. It was therefore decided that we would use the trick with the dummies for just three days, which should give the escapees more than ample time to get well away from the immediate area of the camp. On the fourth morning after the escape our senior officer, who was quite a few ranks higher than the American camp commandant, would officially announce the news of the escape.

This was always followed by the same ritual. Firstly the commandant would give vent to his feelings by loudly cussing us 'damned Krauts'. Then he would get the guards down from the watchtowers and have them locked up (unfortunately, they were invariably the wrong ones). Next he would order the entire camp to be thoroughly searched, for there was always the possibility that the crafty Fritzes had simply gone into hiding and were waiting to escape at their leisure some time later. While all this was going on we were kept out on the parade ground, usually for the remainder of the morning.

Such was our small contribution to the continuing war against the Western allies. But the nearer we got to 1945, the worse the news of the actual war became – and with it the deeper our mood of depression. Our many comrades with families and loved ones still living in Germany's larger towns and cities suffered particularly badly whenever we heard reports of the almost nightly raids by hundreds of British bombers. I was slightly better off in this respect, for our house in Rosenheim was a long way away from the firing line, and none of my close relatives was fighting at the front.

Christmas 1944 in Camp Como was a muted and sombre affair. In the succeeding days our mood was not helped by the realization that the Ardennes counter-offensive was not about to bring the hoped-for change in Germany's fortunes. Even our leaders' long promised and much vaunted 'Wunderwaffen' – first the V1 flying bombs that I had witnessed in England, and now the V2 rocket – were delivering only sporadic pinpricks. Little wonder that our last hopes, pinned on the so-called 'Superwaffe', now began to fade. And when, at the end of January 1945, the Red Army stormed across Germany's eastern borders, an air of fatalism descended over the whole camp.

At last we were being forced to swallow the bitter pill of reality. We knew now that the allies were certain to achieve their stated aim of reducing Germany to total impotence; a nation without power and without a future.

The French were demanding that Germany be split up and divided amongst its neighbours (on the grounds of European hegemony). The Americans and the British advocated implementation of the 1944 Morgenthau Plan, which would reduce Germany to a purely agrarian state (for economic reasons). The Poles, with the support of the Russians (motivated by a mixture of revenge, hatred and expansionism) intended to annex Germany's eastern territories and drive out their ethnic populations.

And over it all hung the allies' insistence on simultaneous unconditional surrender on all fronts.

CHAPTER 9

THE WAR IS OVER

Although we had long accepted that defeat was inevitable, the announcement of Germany's surrender on 8 May 1945 still came as a tremendous blow. But our world really started to come crashing down around our ears when we learned of the atrocities that had been carried out in our name. The American press was full of horrific accounts of the extermination camps discovered by the advancing allies in the closing weeks of the war. A tide of hatred and revulsion was stirred up against anything and everything German.

With the hostilities at an end, the Amis no longer felt obliged to abide by the rules of the Hague Convention. The personal behaviour of the guards towards us remained, as ever, perfectly correct. But as of 9 May 1945 we were taken off the equivalent of US Army rations and placed instead on hunger rations of 800 calories per day.

With typical American attention to meticulous detail, our meals nevertheless continued to consist of all the elements of a 'proper' menu, such as a soup or some other starter, the main course, with vegetables and/or a side salad, and a dessert. But the individual portions of each were so ridiculously miniscule that they reminded me of nothing more than the table set by Snow White for the Seven Dwarfs!

It was only after a couple of weeks, when the first of us began keeling over during morning parade, that the Americans noticed that something was amiss. To their great credit, it must be said that it wasn't in the GIs' nature to treat their prisoners inhumanely and our daily rations were quickly increased to 1,200 calories. This enabled us, if not exactly to thrive, then at least to vegetate in peace and quiet without fear of starvation.

All plans for summer 1945's 'sports term' had to go by the board, of course; we were simply too weak for any sustained physical exercise. I didn't even feel like scraping away at my cello any more. Under the circumstances, I decided to test the validity of the old adage that 'a useful trade always pays good dividends' by volunteering my services as an apprentice baker to the Betriebskompanie. The camp's master baker was the plump and jolly Obergefreiter Katzlberger from Vienna. I'll never forget one piece of good advice he gave me, delivered in his broad Austrian accent: "You've got to knead the dough with as much passion as you would a lovely buxom girl, Herr Leutnant."

The dividends promised by the old saying were duly forthcoming, and my roommates and I soon began to put on a bit of weight and regain our strength. In fact, rations in general were gradually being increased to a more acceptable level. This resulted in an improvement not only in our physical well-being, but also – and this was no doubt the real reason for the Amis' new found generosity – in our mental state. It ensured that we would more easily be able to follow and take in the programme of 're-education' that had been ordered from above.

Our re-educators were German high school professors, some of them of Jewish descent, who had emigrated to the USA before the war. It has to be said that they too were most correct and punctilious in carrying out their duties, the primary purpose of which was to instil in us a proper understanding of democracy and responsible civic behaviour.

The manner in which the discussions were conducted was an absolute eye-opener to me. They were quite open and we were perfectly at liberty to express contrary, even critical points of view without the slightest fear of any reprisal. It was astounding to discover just how many among us – mainly among the older ones – were democrats of long standing who had always been against the Hitler regime.

One of these 'oldies' had a vision for the future that none of us could quite grasp in those still chaotic early post-war days. During one of our re-education discussion sessions he put forward the proposal that the victorious allies should change their policy of punishing Germany into one of forging a new beginning for European politics that would include Germany as an equal partner. He foresaw a kind of 'United States of Europe' with France and Germany together forming its seed crystal. We tapped our foreheads behind his back, suspecting that he had partaken of too many additional calories too quickly.

In actual fact, what we were witnessing was the birth of an idea that was to change the history of Europe in a way that nobody could have possibly imagined at the time. Our 'fantasist' was an Oberleutnant Hallstein, to us just a weedy, even slightly comical figure with glasses perched on the end of his nose and thin legs protruding from a pair of baggy shorts. Ten years later he was Professor Dr. Walter Hallstein, founder of the Hallstein Doctrine and first president of the European Economic Community Commission.

As officer prisoners-of-war we could not be forced to undertake any work for the enemy as long as hostilities were in progress. But now, in the summer of 1945 and with the war between Germany and the Western allies over, we were offered the opportunity to do various kinds of jobs. They were all of a menial nature, of course. But we younger officers jumped at the chance. There was no way of telling how long it would be before we were released and permitted to return home. And quite honestly, despite all the cultural diversions, life at Como was becoming ever more miserable (as for sporting activities, our still far from plentiful diet wouldn't allow for much more than a brisk stroll round the perimeter these days).

And so, in August 1945, almost half of the camp's inmates, a good 400 of us in all, left the state of Mississippi for Winston-Salem in North Carolina, where we were split into a number of smaller working parties. I was one of a group of about thirty POWs who were billeted in a sports hall in the centre of town. The hall, together with a small playing field outside, was surrounded by a high wire fence. Very sensibly, there were no longer any armed guards actively watching over us. But it was made abundantly clear that we were not allowed to go wandering off into town.

It would not have been at all difficult to sneak out of our improvised work camp, but with that tell-tale 'POW' writ large on the backs of our tunics we would have stood out like the proverbial sore thumb. There were compensations, however. We no longer looked out over a dreary wasteland, but on a vista of busy, pulsating everyday America, some aspects of which seemed decidedly strange to our European eyes. From the sports field I can recall being able to see the tower of a nearby church, which had some large letters arranged vertically down much of its length. When darkness fell these lit up in different colours to beseech: 'Jesus save us'.

The town's major employer was – and presumably still is – the R.J. Reynolds Tobacco Company, whose Camel cigarettes were already very familiar to us from Como (although we had been deprived of them since 8 May). When we were told that we would be working in one of the company's branch factories, hopes were raised that we would at last be issued with proper cigarettes again.

We were all sick and tired of trying to roll our own pathetic excuses for cigarettes from the little sacks of loose tobacco that now constituted our ration. This was little more than dust and was, we strongly suspected, the sweepings left over on the factory floor after the cigarette manufacturing process. To our great disappointment we discovered that the factory we worked in didn't actually make cigarettes. It was a fermentation plant for the raw tobacco that came in from Kentucky and other growing areas in huge barrels, some two metres high and one metre in diameter.

Our workplace was a large hall where numbers of black women and girls stood at a sort of conveyor belt pulling apart the tightly compressed bales of raw tobacco and placing the individual leaves on the metal belt that fed them into the fermentation chamber. Our job was to break open the barrels that were stored on wheeled pallets in one corner of the hall and roll the bales of raw tobacco across to the conveyor belt. The work wasn't all that arduous, but we were kept constantly on the go as the nimble fingers of the black girls could pick a bale to pieces in next to no time and we were continually having to replace them.

If we thought we would be permitted to chat to our co-workers, we were very quickly and emphatically advised otherwise; not because it might slow down production, not because we were prisoners-of-war... but because no personal contact of any kind was allowed between white and black.

A lot of the younger girls were extremely attractive, however, and one of our number, whether as a result of long-enforced celibacy or from true feelings of affection, became totally smitten. He managed somehow to convey this to the girl in question and a relationship between the two soon developed. He even built a tiny love nest among the barrels stored in the corner where, hidden behind piles of tobacco leaves, he and his 'inamorata' could snatch a few moments alone.

One day the inevitable happened and the pair were discovered together in their hideaway. Our comrade suffered no punishment, but was simply transferred to another working party. The unfortunate girl did not escape so lightly. She was found guilty of breaking the strict race laws then still in force. In the light of the allies' wartime propaganda on the evils of oppression and our more recent re-education lectures on democracy, the incident left us in a somewhat puzzled frame of mind.

It was not long after this that the various groups of prisoners within the factory were changed around and our party now found itself working in the so-called transport section. Our new job was to unload the large barrels of raw tobacco from the trucks delivering them from the growers, place them on the wheeled pallets and push them into the large storerooms. Physically the work was much harder than before. But it was a lot more relaxed and enjoyable than the rather strained atmosphere within the fermentation hall and, of course, we were outside in the fresh air for most of the time.

Each barrel weighed about eight hundredweight, or some 400 kg, and our early attempts to roll them down off the trucks and then place them upright on the pallets were pretty feeble. The regular workforce, huge muscular negroes to a man, made it seem like child's play. It took just two of them to wrestle a barrel off the truck and load it onto a pallet, while five of us weaklings would be struggling like mad to perform the same task, and risking life and limb in the process. After a little while we too learned the secret, which was to combine strength with momentum. This made the job a lot easier, but we never did manage to do it with anything fewer than three men.

Our foreman was an elderly white man, stockily built, with snow-white hair and a healthy ruddy complexion. We christened him 'Old Gold' after a rival brand of cigarette. Instead of the Reynolds' Camel (actually a dromedary, as one of our more pedantic professors never tired of pointing out), advertisements for the Lorillard Company's Old Gold cigarettes often featured an illustration of a typical American farmer that bore a striking resemblance to our new boss.

At first, this inherently straightforward and friendly character faced a serious dilemma: how to treat these new additions to his work gang. On the one hand, the war was not long over and the reports of atrocities were still fresh in everyone's mind, which surely demanded that he keep his distance. On the other hand, however, his southern upbringing meant that he regarded us not just as Germans but also, and perhaps more importantly from his point of view, as whites.

And this automatically made us much more socially acceptable than his black workers. In the end, I think he reached a compromise in his own mind and at 7am, when it was time to start work, his shout would ring round the yard: "OK! Let's go, boys and niggers!" He was certainly not unsympathetic towards us, he himself had a son who had fought in the war, and in time came to accept our presence completely. Now and again he would even give us a lunchtime treat by handing round some of his wife's – 'Mom's' – home-made cakes.

The drivers of the delivery trucks proved equally generous. After a while they entrusted us with the job of removing and folding up the large tarpaulins that covered their loads. The results of our labours were rarely as neat and tidy as they might have been, but we would each be rewarded with a pack of Camels all the same. And if we had thought that the little drawstring sacks of dusty sweepings that constituted our official tobacco issue was an inferior product only good enough for us, we were astounded to discover that some of the truckers actually preferred it. One of the drivers even had the extraordinary knack of being able to roll himself a cigarette with his hands in his pockets!

But our Old Gold didn't hold with manufactured tobacco products of any kind whatsoever. His liked his tobacco raw. Whenever he felt like it, he would simply tease a wad of compressed leaves out of a gap between the staves of one of the barrels, pop it into his mouth and start chewing. The amount of saliva this habit produced was phenomenal. He would spit frequently and copiously, and could hit a target several metres away with amazing accuracy.

It was an education to watch him on those occasions when he rolled up his sleeves and lent us a hand. This usually happened when, for some reason or another, we couldn't get a barrel on to a pallet and had to roll it along the ground. The damned things were almost uncontrollable and we would be veering about all over the place. That was when he would take over. He would bound along, his great mitts guiding the barrel as straight as a dye, letting fly with gobbets of brown tobacco juice to left and right every five metres. It was said that if you couldn't find him, all you had to do was follow his trail.

Our time with the transport section finally came to an end. Although the work had been hard, the friendly atmosphere had made it a far from unpleasant experience. Unfortunately, the same could not be said of our next – and final – place of employment in the United States, which proved to be something of a major disappointment. It was not that we were treated badly. It was just that we had been transferred to an artificial fertilizer manufacturing plant and the conditions were, to put it mildly, pretty horrific.

Even at first sight the place had a neglected and rundown appearance. It was just a bare patch of ground dominated by a very large, but very dilapidated wooden building. Inside it was no better. High up in the barn-like structure, just below the roof beams, ran a narrow-gauge track. There was no flooring of any kind between the sleepers, or ties, and no guardrails at either side. Incredibly, men were pushing tipper trucks, presumably containing the various ingredients of the fertilizer mix, along this rickety track and emptying their contents from above into seven triangular-shaped silos. It was certainly no job for anyone who suffered from giddiness, but would have provided ideal employment for an out of work circus high-wire walker.

To our great relief, we were not sent up into the roof, but were allowed to keep our feet firmly on the ground – quite literally, for the floor of the barn was just bare earth. In front of each silo stood a wheelbarrow. Our task was to fill the barrow with whatever stuff that particular silo contained and then push it across to a weighing machine. Here, according to the final mixture required, the black foreman would add ingredients from one or more of the seven little piles of unidentified substances that surrounded him. Then the barrow would have to be pushed to a trap in the floor and its contents tipped into the underground mixing and bagging machine.

The whole process resembled some idiotic human conveyor belt as we pushed our wheelbarrows at the double from silo to weighing machine to trapdoor and back to silo again. The black foreman kept us on the move without pause. We had nicknamed him 'Knickebein' – 'Knock-knees' – by the way, as he had been wounded in both knees during the First World War and walked with a peculiar knock-kneed gait.

But what we suffered from most of all was the pungent, evil-smelling dust that hung permanently in the air inside the barn. It formed a constant all-pervading cloud. And without face-masks we could not avoid breathing it in. The company's black employees, who had been working there for years and no doubt still had years of the same ahead of them, were completely unaware of the danger this posed to their health.

Our protests on site had no effect whatsoever. So we lodged an official complaint via our camp administration with the Red Cross. Amazingly, this produced almost immediate results. Not only did representatives of the Red Cross turn up at the factory, so too did a commission from the workers' own union. The validity of our complaints was demonstrated in dramatic fashion even as the gentlemen of the commission were gathered in a corner of the barn discussing the situation.

With a blood-curdling scream, one of the workers pushing a tipper truck high in the roof fell from the overhead rails. It looked terrible. But, in fact, it wasn't as bad as it seemed. He landed on top of the softest and highest of the many piles of fertilizer mix scattered about the factory floor. Even so, the hoped-for improvements failed to materialize. No planking was laid between the ties of the tracks up in the roof. No guardrails were fitted. And no facemasks were issued.

But for us, at any rate, the matter soon became academic. For after about six weeks of hard labour in this 'lung clinic' it was officially announced that we were in line for repatriation. Our excitement can be imagined. Letters containing the tidings of joy were quickly despatched home. Among those I informed were the Schlossmann family on their Hubertus farmstead in South Africa whom, for safety's sake, I addressed as 'Uncle and Aunt'.

At the end of April 1946 things started to happen. With a group of about another 100 prisoners we were put on a train back to New York. But this time there were no armed guards, locked carriages or closed windows – nor, sadly, any delicious meals in station restaurants served by wide-eyed black waitresses.

If I remember rightly, it was on 1 May 1946 that our American adventure ended where it had begun, in New York harbour, with our boarding the ship that was to ferry us back across the

Atlantic to Europe. Here too things were very different from the outward crossing. We weren't cooped up in cabins behind barbed wire, but were allowed to stroll around on deck, which we did for almost the entire crossing.

This time, however, the captain didn't welcome us aboard as 'guests of the United States Navy', for we were no longer classified as officer prisoners-of-war. Now, according to an American Joint Chiefs of Staff ruling of April 1945 (JCS 1067: 4b), we were regarded as members of a 'conquered enemy nation'.

Not worrying a great deal about our official status and what label had been pinned on us, we spent our days up on deck getting to know many of the other prisoners we had not come into contact with before. We had lengthy discussions about what the future held, both for us personally and for our country. These sometimes got quite heated. Most of us were convinced that we would be released immediately upon arrival and sent straight home.

But there were some nasty rumours going around to the effect that German prisoners – as we still considered ourselves – were being sent to a temporary camp in France and there 'auctioned off' for further labour in either France or England. After about ten days we docked at Le Havre in France. From here we were taken first to the tented encampment of Bolbeque not far from the port.

The camp was a very primitive place with a bad reputation. And rightly so, for it now transpired that the shipboard rumours were at least partially true. Bolbeque served not only as a transit camp for those going on to Marburg, north of Frankfurt, to be released. It was also a redistribution centre where prisoners arriving from America were being handed over to the British or French for further terms of captivity working, for example, in coalmines or stone quarries.

My cousin Ingo was one such unfortunate who underwent several more years in the hands of the British. But I was luckier. After just a couple of weeks spent in the damp and unhealthy conditions of Bolbeque, where we slept on blankets on the bare ground, I was sent to Marburg for release.

And it was here, on 27 June 1946, that I spent the last of the 2,388 days of my military career.

Reports in the American papers had prepared me to some extent for the changed conditions I would find in Germany. But it was not until I experienced them for myself that I realized just how totally different the country had become. The town of Marburg had suffered very little bomb damage during the war. But even here, during the few hours between my release from camp and the departure of my train for Rosenheim, I was struck by the almost empty shop windows, the shabby appearance of the people in the streets, who were mostly either elderly or the very young, and – of course – the bored-looking GIs lounging about on the street corners chewing gum.

It was a total shock how everything that I had simply taken for granted during my last home leave in 1943 – everything that had made Germany what it was – had gone to such rack and ruin.

At Marburg railway station I had to push and shove my way through a dense and milling throng of people of every kind to get to the Rosenheim train, which was standing at the platform already packed with passengers but with yet more fighting and struggling to get on board. The journey must have taken a good ten hours and I had to stand the whole way. Whenever we stopped at a station I had literally to fight to keep my place as even more people tried to climb on to the train. At one of the larger stations a young woman did exactly that – she 'climbed' on board.

After throwing her bundle of belongings in through the open

window, she clambered up the side of the carriage. Rough hands pushed her from the outside and pulled her from the inside. To a barrage of coarse remarks she managed to wriggle her way in through the window. She had almost made it, with only her feet still sticking out, when someone on the crowded platform snatched off her shoes and disappeared into the mass of people.

It might all sound terribly funny today. But for the distraught young woman back then it was a catastrophe. In those post-war months items such as shoes were well nigh irreplaceable. Even if she did have enough coupons, and the cash, to buy a new pair –which was most unlikely – there were none to be had in the shops. Her only other option would be to pay the horrendous prices being asked on the black market.

As we were drawing in to Munich's main station I had already spotted the smashed dome of the ministry of transport building in Arnulfstrasse off to my left. But I wasn't prepared for the scene of utter desolation that then confronted me. The Munich whose intact and immaculate streets, squares and ornamental gardens I remembered so well was no more. In its place there stretched a desolate waste of ruins and rubble. I couldn't wait for the train to pull out again and put it all behind me.

From mother's letters I knew that Rosenheim had suffered hardly at all from the allied bombing. Our house had been hit by a single incendiary that had smashed through the canopy roof without causing any serious damage. So it was with an understandable feeling of joy mixed with excitement that I clambered off the train at Rosenheim and set off along the familiar streets to our family home.

After three long years' absence I was finally back, almost choking with emotion as I took my mother, grandmother and sister in my arms. Thank God they had all come through those intervening years fit, well and almost unharmed. The only casualty was my sister, who had a relatively minor wound in her shin, the result of being shot at by a low-flying American fighter while out skiing.

In order to re-establish my identity and be able simply to exist in post-war Germany, I had to become a registered individual. So the next thing to do was to make my way to the local authority offices at Westerndorf-Sankt Peter. Here, upon production of my official discharge papers, I was issued with ration and clothing coupons and suchlike. The old Reichsmark was still the country's sole legal tender, but it could only be used for shop purchases in conjunction with the necessary coupons.

Without these, people had to resort to the flourishing black market with its hugely inflated prices. The fixed unit of currency for most illegal transactions (apart from the US Dollar, of course) were 'Ami-cigarettes', which had a street value of five Reichsmarks each. Whenever I saw a single Camel or Lucky Strike changing hands, my mind automatically went back to the R.J. Reynolds factory in Winston-Salem where I had been working just a year earlier. If only I had kept a few of those packs of cigarettes that the delivery drivers had so casually tossed my way!

In an effort to save on clothing coupons, mother 'converted' my old Luftwaffe uniform, which the Staffel had sent back to her after I had been shot down. The end result was an outfit combining military and civilian items in one fetching ensemble. Such apparel – a sports jacket with breeches and knee boots, for example – was commonly known as 'Räuberzivil', literally 'robber civvies'. It was the height of fashion in Germany in the immediate post-war period and was what nearly every well-dressed young man was wearing that season.

The next important step was a visit to the so-called 'Spruchkammer', or 'judgement chamber', to find out if, by any chance, I could be officially 'denazified'. For this purpose I was handed a questionnaire about a metre long, which I was in-

MILITARY GOVERNMENT OF GERMANY
Fragebogen

WARNING: Read the entire Fragebogen carefully before you start to fill it out. The English language will prevail if discrepancies exist between it and the German translation. Answers must be typewritten or printed clearly in block letters. Every question must be answered precisely and conscientiously and no space is to be left blank. If a question is to be answered by either "yes" or "no", print the word "yes" or "no" in the appropriate space. If the question is inapplicable, so indicate by some appropriate word or phrase such as "none" or "not applicable". Add supplementary sheets if there is not enough space in the questionnaire. Omissions or false or incomplete statements are offenses against Military Government and will result in prosecution and punishment.

WARNUNG: Vor Beantwortung ist der gesamte Fragebogen sorgfältig durchzulesen. In Zweifelsfällen ist die englische Fassung maßgebend. Die Antworten müssen mit der Schreibmaschine oder in klaren Blockbuchstaben geschrieben werden. Jede Frage ist genau und gewissenhaft zu beantworten und keine Frage darf unbeantwortet gelassen werden. Das Wort „Ja" oder „Nein" ist an der jeweilig vorgeschenen Stelle unbedingt einzusetzen. Falls die Frage durch „Ja" oder „Nein" nicht zu beantworten ist, so ist eine entsprechende Antwort, wie z. B. „keine" oder „nicht betreffend" zu geben. In Ermangelung von ausreichendem Platz in dem Fragebogen können Bogen angeheftet werden. Auslassungen sowie falsche oder unvollständige Angaben stellen Vergehen gegen die Verordnungen der Militärregierung dar und werden dementsprechend geahndet.

A. PERSONAL / A. Persönliche Angaben

1. List position for which you are under consideration (include agency or firm). — 2. Name (Surname). (Fore Names). — 3. Other names which you have used or by which you have been known. — 4. Date of birth. — 5. Place of birth. — 6. Height. — 7. Weight. — 8. Color of hair. — 9. Color of eyes. — 10. Scars, marks or deformities. — 11. Present address (City, street and house number). — 12. Permanent residence (City, street and house number). — 13. Identity card type and Number. — 14. Wehrpaß No. — 15. Passport No. — 16. Citizenship. — 17. If a naturalized citizen, give date and place of naturalization. — 18. List any titles of nobility ever held by you or your wife or by the parents or grandparents of either of you. — 19. Religion. 20. With what church are you affiliated? — 21. Have you ever severed your connection with any church, officially or unofficially? — 22. If so, give particulars and reason. — 23. What religious preference did you give in the census of 1939? — 24. List any crimes of which you have been convicted, giving dates, locations and nature of the crimes. —

1. Für Sie in Frage kommende Stellung: *Werbewalter*

2. Name *Fischer* *Wolfgang* 3. Andere von Ihnen benutzte Namen

    (Familien)-name   (Vornamé)-name *Klaus*

oder solche, unter welchen Sie bekannt sind

4. Geburtsdatum *30.X.1921* 5. Geburtsort *Waldthürn*

6. Größe *1.78 mts.* 7. Gewicht *65 Kg.* 8. Haarfarbe *braun* 9. Farbe der Augen *grau*

Narben, Geburtsmale oder Entstellungen *Keine*

11. Gegenwärtige Anschrift *Rosenheim Obb. Hofbräukeller 37*

    (Stadt, Straße und Hausnummer)

12. Ständiger Wohnsitz *Rosenheim Obb. Hofbräukeller 37*

    (Stadt, Straße und Hausnummer)

13. Art der Ausweiskarte *Kennkarten-D 55152* 14. Wehrpaß-Nr. *Unbekannt* 15. Reisepaß-Nr. *keinen*

16. Staatsangehörigkeit *Deutsch* 17. Falls naturalisierter Bürger, geben Sie Datum und Einbürgerungsort

an *nicht zutreffend*

18. Aufzählung Ihrerseits oder seitens Ihrer Ehefrau oder Ihrer beiden Großeltern innegehabten Adelstitel

nicht zutreffend

19. Religion *evangelisch* 20. Welcher Kirche gehören Sie an? *evangelische* 21. Haben Sie je offiziell oder inoffiziell Ihre Verbindung mit einer Kirche aufgelöst? *Nein* 22. Falls ja, geben Sie Einzelheiten und Gründe an

nicht betreffend 23. Welche Religionsangehörigkeit haben Sie bei der Volkszählung 1939 angegeben? *evangelisch* 24. Führen Sie alle Vergehen, Uebertretungen oder Verbrechen an, für welche Sie je verurteilt worden sind, mit Angaben des Datums, des Ortes und der Art

nicht betreffend

B. SECONDARY AND HIGHER EDUCATION / B. Grundschul- und höhere Bildung

Name and Type of School (If a special Nazi school or military academy, so specify) / Name und Art der Schule (Im Fall r besonderen NS oder Militärakademie geben Sie dies an)	Location / Ort	Dates of Attendance / Wann besucht?	Certificate Diploma or Degree / Zeugnis, Diplom o. akademischer Grad	Did Abitur permit University matriculation? / Berechtigt Abitur od. Reifezeugnis zur Universitäts-immatrikulation?	Date / Datum
Hum. Gymnasium	*Rosenheim*	*1931–1939*	*Abitür*	*ja*	*15.11.1939*

25. List any German University Student Corps to which you have ever belonged. — 26. List (giving location and dates) any Napola, Adolf Hitler School, Nazi Leaders College or military academy in which you have ever been a teacher. — 27. Have your children ever attended any of such schools? If so, where and when? — 28. List (giving location and dates) any school in which you have ever been a Vertrauenslehrer (formerly Jugendwalter).

25. Welchen deutschen Universitäts-Studentenburschenschaften haben Sie je angehört? *Keine*

26. In welchen Napola, Adolf-Hitler-, NS-Führerschulen oder Militärakademien waren Sie je Lehrer? Anzugeben mit genauer Orts- und Zeitbestimmung *Keine*

27. Haben Ihre Kinder eine der obengenannten Schulen besucht? *Nein* Welche, wo und wann?

nicht betreffend

28. Führen Sie (mit Orts- und Zeitbestimmung) alle Schulen an, in welchen Sie je Vertrauenslehrer (vormalig Jugendwalter) waren *nicht zutreffend*

C. PROFESSIONAL OR TRADE EXAMINATIONS / C. Berufs- oder Handwerksprüfungen

Name of Examination / Name der Prüfung	Place Taken / Ort	Result / Resultat	Date / Datum
nicht betreffend			

The first page of the lengthy questionnaire that officially 'denazified' one Fischer, Wolfgang, and readmitted him to polite society.

187

structed to complete in full. Thanks to my uncomplicated and non-political background, this posed few problems. After long deliberation and rigorous checking, I was duly informed that I could consider myself herewith denazified as part of the general youth amnesty. I felt like pointing out that a glance at my date of birth could have saved us all a whole lot of time and trouble.

Slowly life returned to what passed for normal in those days. And once again I found myself drawn to the banks of the Inn. It was early summer and the river, swollen by the snowmelt high in the Alps, was still in almost full spate; its roaring and tumbling progress music to my ears. I would sit there for hours, watching the sandy-coloured mass of water rushing past just below my feet, carrying with it twigs, branches, sometimes even whole tree trunks.

After my 10,000-kilometre odyssey to the mighty Mississippi and back, I was at long last home again. Home to my family and to my beloved River Inn – timeless and untouched by the pettiness, the politics and the wars of man.

APPENDIX 1

AIRCRAFT TYPES FLOWN BY THE AUTHOR

Type	Description	Unit
Grunau G9	Training glider	Flieger-Hitler-jugend
Zögling 33	Training glider	Flieger-Hitler-jugend
Grunau Baby	Training glider	Flieger-Hitler-jugend
Focke-Wulf Fw 44 Stieglitz	Basic trainer	Luftkriegsschule 4
Bücker Bü 131 Jungmann	Basic trainer	Luftkriegsschule 4
	Basic trainer	Jagdlehrerüber-prüfungsgruppe
Arado Ar 66	Basic trainer	Luftkriegsschule 4
	Basic trainer	Jagdgeschwader 107
	Blind-flying trainer	Jagdgeschwader 110
Bücker Bü 181 Bestmann	Trainer	Luftkriegsschule 4
Focke-Wulf Fw 56 Stösser	Aerobatic trainer	Luftkriegsschule 4
	Aerobatic trainer	Jagdgeschwader 107

Arado Ar 96	Advanced trainer	Luftkriegsschule 4
	Advanced trainer	Jagdgeschwader 107
Heinkel He 51	Fighter trainer	Luftkriegsschule 4
Messerschmitt Me 109D	Fighter trainer	Jagdgeschwader 107
Messerschmitt Me 109E	Fighter trainer	Jagdgeschwader 107
Messerschmitt Me 109F	Fighter trainer	Jagdgeschwader 107
	Fighter trainer	Jagdlehrerüber- prüfungsgruppe
Messerschmitt Me 109G	Fighter trainer	Jagdgeschwader 107
	Fighter trainer	Jagdlehrerüber- prüfungsgruppe
	Blind-flying trainer	Jagdgeschwader 110
Bloch 151	Fighter trainer (ex-FAF)	Jagdgeschwader 107
Dewoitine D.520	Fighter trainer (ex-FAF)	Jagdgeschwader 107
Potez 63	Multi-engined trainer (ex-FAF)	Jagdgeschwader 107
North American NAA-64	Advanced trainer (ex-FAF)	Jagdgeschwader 107
Supermarine Spitfire	(Familiarization /ex-RAF)	Jagdgeschwader 107
Focke-Wulf Fw 190A	Fighter trainer	Jagdlehrerüber- prüfungsgruppe

AIRCRAFT TYPES FLOWN BY THE AUTHOR

Gotha Go 145	Blind-flying trainer	Jagdgeschwader 110
Messerschmitt Me 109G-6	Operational fighter	I./JG 2 (4. Staffel)
Focke-Wulf Fw 190A-8	Operational fighter	I./JG 2 (3. Staffel)

APPENDIX 2
UNITS IN
WHICH THE AUTHOR SERVED

Unit	Duty	Location	Period
Fliegeraus-bildungs-regiment 33	Basic training	Manching Königsberg Elbing	Nov 1939 – Feb 1940
Aufklärugs-gruppe (F)/Ob.d.L.	General duties	Brüsterort Döberitz	Feb 1940 – Aug 1940
Wetterzentrale XII (mot.)	Meteorological clerk	Étampes Deauville-Trouville Villacoublay	Sept 1940 – Feb 1941
Fliegerhorst-kompanie Villacoublay	General duties	Villacoublay	Feb 1941 – June 1941
Unteroffiziers-lehrkurs	NCO training	Neukuhren	July 1941 – Aug 1941
Fliegerhorst-kompanie Villacoublay	NCO duties	Villacoublay	Sept 1941 – Jan 1942
Luftkriegs-schule 4	Flying training	Fürstenfeld-bruck Bad Wöris-hofen	Feb 1942 – Jan 1943
Jagdge-schwader 107	Fighter training	Nancy-Essay	Feb 1943 – June 1943
Jagdge-schwader 107	Fighter instructor	Nancy-Essay	July 1943 – Sep 1943

UNITS IN WHICH THE AUTHOR SERVED

Jagdlehrerüber-prüfungs-gruppe	Instructor training	Guyancourt Aix-en-Provence	Oct 1943 – Dec 1943
Jagdgeschwader 110	Blind-flying training	Altenburg	Jan 1944 – Feb 1944
1./Ergänzungs-jagdgruppe West	Operational training	Liegnitz	Feb 1944
4./Jagdge-schwader 2 Richthofen	Operational	Aix-en-Provence Canino / Italy	Mar 1944 – Apr 1944
3./Jagdge-schwader 2 Richthofen	Operational	Aix-en-Provence Cormeilles Boissy Nancy Creil Senlis	Apr 1944 – June 19444
British captivity	POW	Vers-sur-Mer Preston Beaconsfield Derby	June 1944 – July 1944
US captivity	POW	Como/Miss. Winston-Salem /NC Bolbeque (Fr)	July 1944 – June 1946

APPENDIX 3

UNIT NOTES
AND HISTORIES

1: Fliegerausbildungsregiment 33 *(Initial Training Regiment 33)*

When the Luftwaffe was created in the mid-'thirties the basic training of new recruits was carried out by the so-called Fliegerersatzabteilungen (literally 'air personnel replacement departments'). There were six such establishments; one located in each of the six Luftkreise, or air territorial regions, into which Germany was divided.

By 1 April 1939, when the original Fliegerersatzabteilungen (FEAs) were redesignated as Fliegerausbildungsregimenter (FARs = initial [air] training regiments), their numbers had grown to twenty-six.One of these was Fliegerausbildungsregiment 33, whose numerical designation indicated that it was the third such regiment to be activated within the area of Luftflotte (Air Fleet) 3.

By this time too the FARs had each been organized into two component battalions: the first (the original FEA) providing basic training and the second being an initial flying training school. It was customary for a new recruit, having successfully completed his basic military training with the first battalion, then to progress to the same unit's second to commence flying training.

The original intention had been to activate FAR 33 at Darmstadt. But when it was decided that this field lacked the necessary facilities, the regiment was set up instead at Ingolstadt, north of Munich, with a satellite station at Dornstadt near Ulm. Commanded by Oberst Heinrich Geerkens, FAR 33 was transferred in November 1939 to Königsberg in East Prussia, with flying training being carried out at nearby Elbing.

In 1941 came the parting of the ways for FAR 33's two battalions. The basic training battalion moved to Detmold, SE of Osnabrück. Here, in the winter of 1942/43, it was redesignated Jäger-Regiment (L) 33 – Luftwaffe Rifle Regiment 33 – to become part of the newly forming 17. Luftwaffen-Feld-Division. This unit, one of twenty-two such infantry divisions made up of Luftwaffe personnel, was transferred to Le Havre on the French channel coast in February 1943.

Commanded since November 1943 by the army's Generalleutnant Erich Höcker, the division was virtually annihilated in August 1944 during the fighting in northern France following the D-Day invasion. The surviving remnants were subsequently incorporated into the 167. Volksgrenadier-Division.

Meanwhile, back in March 1941, the second battalion – i.e. the initial flying training school (Sch./FAR 33) – had itself been redesignated to become Flugzeugführerschule A/B 123 (FFS A/B 123 = pilots' school [single-engined] 123), moving two months later to Agram (now Zagreb) in Croatia.

A new FFS A/B 33 was immediately formed by redesignating the existing FFS A/B 5. This flying school, commanded by Oberstleutnant (later Oberst) Walter Milz, was first based at Quakenbrück, north of Osnabrück, with satellite stations at Plantlünne, Hopsten and Diepholz. The latter field was used for night-flying training, which began to play an ever more important role in the school's curriculum after its transfer to Altenburg in Thuringia in the summer of 1942.

Finally, early in May 1943, FFS A/B 33 was redesignated as a specialized night and blind-flying school: Blindflugschule 10 (BFS 10). For further details see JG 110 below.

2: Aufklärungsgruppe (F)/Ob.d.L. (*Strategic Reconnaissance Group of the Luftwaffe High Command*)
Although not officially designated as such until 1939, the Aufklärungsgruppe (F)/Ob.d.L. could trace its origins back to the earliest days of the then still secret Luftwaffe. Formed from part of the Fliegerstaffel zbV (special-purposes air squadron) first activated on 1 January 1935, the High Command's special reconnaissance unit came into being at Berlin-Staaken under the covert title of the Flugbereitschaft Abteilung B (Duty Flight Department B).

Initially equipped with just two single-engined Junkers aircraft (a Ju W 34fue and a Ju F 13), the unit was soon given a slightly more transparent cover designation. Operating as the Versuchsstelle für Höhenflüge (test centre for high-altitude flight), it received examples of some of the latest twin-engined machines entering Luftwaffe service in the latter half of the 'thirties, including the Dornier Do 17, Heinkel He 111 and Junkers Ju 86.

More commonly referred to as the Kommando Rowehl (after its long-standing CO, the later Oberstleutnant Theodor Rowehl), the unit undertook many top-secret photo-reconnaissance missions in the months leading up to World War II.

Comprising just two Staffeln upon the outbreak of hostilities in September 1939, the Gruppe was doubled in strength the following month when two existing long-range reconnaissance units, 8.(F)/LG 2 and 2.(F)/121, were redesignated to become its 3. and 4. Staffeln respectively. Still headquartered in Berlin, but with its component units operating from a succession of outlying bases, including Brüsterort, Fritzlar and Norkitten, the Aufkl.Gr (F)/Ob.d.L. continued its clandestine activities during the early years of the war, flying high-altitude photographic reconnaissance missions over areas of future conflict such as France, Great Britain and the Soviet Union. The aerial photographs its aircraft brought back often provided the basis for the target maps later issued to the Luftwaffe's bomber crews.

By the beginning of 1942, however, with the need for such operations declining, the Gruppenstab of the Aufkl.Gr (F)/Ob.d.L. was disbanded and its four component Staffeln were redeployed to serve as standard long-range reconnaissance units on the eastern front. In January 1943 1., 2. and 3.(F)/Ob.d.L. were then redesignated to form a new strategic reconnaissance Gruppe: Aufkl.Gr (F)/100. And two months after that 4.(F)/Ob.d.L. was incorporated into the High Command's Versuchsverband (test and experimental unit).

3: Wetterzentrale XII (mot.) *(Meteorological Centre XII [mob.])*

Despite the 'mot.' in its title (indicating 'motorisiert' or 'mobile'), Wetterzentrale XII was one of a number of semi-permanent Luftwaffe stations set up to receive and decipher meteorological reports. For in addition to its own dedicated Wettererkundungsstaffeln (meteorological squadrons), the Luftwaffe also relied on reports from various other sources, including long-range reconnaissance aircraft (primarily the Focke-Wulf Fw 200 Condor maritime reconnaissance bomber), ships at sea, both Axis and neutral, and land-based weather stations such as those the Germans had been able to establish above the Arctic Circle on Greenland and Spitsbergen.

These provided vital information to the planners of the various air commands. In Wetterzentrale XII's case this command was Luftflotte 3, headquartered in Paris and one of the two major air fleets involved in the Battle of Britain and the subsequent night Blitz on Great Britain.

4: Fliegerhorstkompanie Villacoublay *(Villacoublay Airfield Permanent Base Company)*

The Luftwaffe's operational bases were staffed on three separate levels. The ground personnel of the resident flying unit(s) were responsible for the maintenance and servicing of their aircraft and all matters relating thereto. Each airfield also had its own Flughafenbetriebskompanie (airfield servicing company), normally comprising three-four platoons, whose task was the upkeep and repair of the runway, buildings and all other facilities on the base (in RAF parlance: 'works'n bricks'). Then came the permanent staff under the Fliegerhorstkommandant (station commander), whose responsibility was the day-to-day running of the base, including administration, discipline, stores, security and the like.

An Armée de l'Air fighter base at the beginning of the war, Villacoublay was taken over by the Luftwaffe immediately after the French surrender of June 1940; initially housing all 100-plus Heinkel He 111 bombers of Kampfgeschwader 55 during the opening phase of the Battle of Britain. The next four years saw a miscellany of flying units occupying the base. By the summer of 1944 and the invasion of Normandy, the aircraft operating out of the extended Villacoublay complex were the Me 109 fighters of III./JG 26 and the Fw 190s of III./JG 54. Their withdrawal in mid-August 1944 in the face of the advancing allies marked the end of the Luftwaffe's tenure of the base and its return to French hands.

5: Unteroffizierslehrkurs Neukuhren *(NCOs' training course, Neukuhren)*

The two-month instructional courses for NCOs, such as those conducted at Neukuhren in East Prussia and elsewhere in the Reich, were a regular and integral part of the promotion process for other ranks and officer aspirants in the Luftwaffe.

6: Luftkriegsschule 4 (Air Warfare School 4)

Opened on 1 October 1937 as the Luftkriegsschule Fürstenfeld-bruck under the command of Generalmajor Ritter und Edler Hermann von Mann, this school remained *in situ* for just over two years before, in November 1939, the exigencies of war necessitated its temporary transfer to Königsberg in East Prussia. In its absence Fürstenfeldbruck was used first to house the Heinkel He 111 bombers of Kampfgeschwader 51, and then as a test centre by the Dornier aircraft company.

In January 1940, while the unit was still based at Königsberg (with outstations at Eichwalde, Gutenfeld and Schippenbeil), the seven air warfare schools – hitherto identified solely by their place of origin – were given numerical designations. The unit thus returned to Fürstenfeldbruck in mid-August 1940 as Luftkriegsschule 4. Here it would continue to operate until early 1945. During this time, commanded in turn by Generalmajors Herbert Sonnenburg (1940-43) and Otto Höhne (1943-45), it utilized a large number of satellite fields, including Munich-Oberwiesenfeld, Bad Wörishofen, Kempten-Durach, Puchhof, Schongau, Leipheim, Neu-Ulm and Landsberg/Lech (the last named for glider training).

At the beginning of 1945 training was terminated due to the then chronic shortage of aviation fuel. The members of the final officer candidates' course were initially earmarked to serve as infantry in the defence of Berlin, but were instead amalgamated into the 29. and 30. Fallschirmjäger-Regiment currently based at Graz in Austria. These two parachute regiments were part of Generalleutnant Gustav Wilke's newly forming 10. Fallschirmjäger-Division.

Although the Luftwaffe's parachute forces had not been employed as such in any strength since the disastrous Cretan campaign of May 1941, Göring had refused to have them disbanded and they had since acquired a formidable reputation as ground troops. In the closing days of the war the two regiments were thrown into the hopeless battle trying to stop the Red Army's advance into Austria: 29. being deployed in the Vienna area and 30. to the southeast of Graz.

7: Jagdgeschwader 107 (Fighter [Training] Wing 107)

In October 1942 Major Georg Meyer's Zerstörervorschule 1 (Zerstörer Preliminary School 1), which had been activated at Nancy-Essay three months earlier, was there redesignated to become Jagdfliegerschule 7 (Fighter Pilots' School 7). Late in January 1943 the school then underwent another change of designation to emerge as Jagdgeschwader 107.

The Luftwaffe's seventeen three-digit Jagdgeschwader (JGs 101-117) were all training, and not operational units. But although termed a Geschwader, JG 107 in fact consisted of just one single Gruppe made up of three Staffeln. Major Meyer was nonetheless appointed to the post of Geschwaderkommodore, with Hauptmann Franz Hörnig, who had hitherto served as Meyer's deputy, becoming the Gruppenkommandeur of I./JG 107.

With the exception of 2. Staffel, which was deployed to Toul, the unit remained at Nancy-Essay throughout the whole of 1943 and into 1944. By the spring of 1944, however, marauding allied fighter-bombers were beginning to make their presence felt in JG 107's training areas around Nancy. But it was the bombing raid by B-17 Flying Fortresses of the 8th USAF on the airfield itself on 25 April 1944 that finally forced the school to vacate Nancy-Essay. The Me 109 component retired to Fürth on 2 May. Five days later the remainder of the school was transferred, via Markersdorf, to Börgönd and Tapolca in Hungary, where it was redesignated as II./JG 108. As such it was disbanded in Austria early in 1945 and its personnel remustered as infantry.

Meanwhile, another JG 107 had been set up in October 1944

at Hagenow, southwest of Schwerin, under the command of Oberstleutnant Hennig Strümpell. (A veteran of the *Legion Condor*, with whom he had scored his first two victories during the Spanish Civil War, the then Hauptmann Strümpell had subsequently commanded I./JG 2 Richthofen during the opening weeks of the Battle of Britain.) At this late stage of the war, the original plan to employ the 'new' JG 107 as a blind-flying school had to be abandoned due to shortages of technical equipment, qualified instructors and suitable aircraft. I./JG 107 was thus never fully activated.

A second Gruppe, II./JG 107 (the ex-JG 116), did manage to undertake some perfunctory day-fighter training at Hildesheim, southeast of Hannover, for just over two months during the winter of 1944/45 before it too was disbanded in February 1945.

8: Jagdlehrerüberprüfungsgruppe *(Fighter Instructors' Inspection Group)*

The growing need for fighter pilots and the consequent proliferation of fighter training schools to meet this need had, in turn, resulted in an increased demand for qualified fighter instructors. In October 1941 Jagdfliegerschule 5 (Fighter Pilots' School 5), then based at Bernay in France, set up a fifth Staffel (5./JFS 5) specifically for the purpose of training instructors.

A year later, on 1 September 1942, this Staffel was retitled the Jagdlehrerüberprüfungsstelle (fighter instructors' inspection centre). It moved from Bernay to Orléans-Bricy under the command of Oberleutnant Erich Hohagen (a later Gruppenkommandeur of I./JG 2 Richthofen). In November a Gruppenstab was formed, which led to the unit's undergoing another minor change of designation to become the Jagdlehrerüberprüfungsgruppe.

The Gruppe remained at Orléans-Bricy until the end of August 1943. The instructors' test courses, which had lasted anything from two to four weeks in the days of 5./JFS 5, were now extended to two months. During the summer of 1943 the Gruppe also operated a so-called Einsatzschwarm (an operational formation of four machines). Its task was to defend the airspace around Orléans, and later around Paris, against incursions by allied aircraft.

On 1 September 1943 the Gruppe moved to Guyancourt near Paris, before then deploying to the more peaceful skies of Orange-Caritat in the south of France towards the end of the year. During the winter months of 1943/44 the Gruppe's pilots flew patrols over the Mediterranean from Orange, as well as from the unit's satellite fields at Marseilles and Aix. Then in the spring of 1944, with the threat of an allied invasion of southern France looming large, the Gruppe exchanged the Mediterranean for the Baltic, taking up residence at Garz/Usedom where, on 1 June 1944, it was redesignated to become II./JG 110 (see below).

9: Jagdgeschwader 110 *(Fighter [Training] Wing 110)*

In May 1943 the flying training school based at Altenburg in Thuringia, FFS A/B 33 (see above), was redesignated as Blindflugschule 10 (Blind-Flying School 10). Remaining at Altenburg, with a satellite field at Pommsen in Saxony, the school – commanded by Oberstleutnant Max Gerstenberger and re-equipped with new Me 109s and Fw 109s – was specifically tasked with the training of pilots for single-engined Wilde Sau night-fighter operations.

On 15 October the unit provided the nucleus (I. Gruppe) for the newly forming Jagdgeschwader 110. Oberstleutnant Gerstenberger was appointed to be the Geschwaderkommodore, with Hauptmann Albert Falderbaum becoming the Gruppenkommandeur of I./JG 110. The Gruppe continued its Wilde Sau training activities as before. It also sent small detachments of instructors to many of the day fighter Gruppen engaged in

Defence of the Reich operations to teach their pilots rudimentary blind-flying techniques.

In June 1944 JG 110 was increased in strength by the incorporation of the Garz-based Jagdlehrerüberprüfungsgruppe (see above), which was redesignated to become II./JG 110. The new designation did not mean a change of role, however. The new Gruppe was still concerned solely with the training and testing of flying instructors.

The following month, July 1944, a multi-engined night-flying training school of long standing, FFS B 36 (first activated at Radom in Poland back in October 1940), ceased operations as such and was redesignated III./JG 110. Re-equipped with single-seaters, it began to train newly qualified fighter pilots in blind and bad-weather flying.

I./JG 110 moved from Altenburg to Brunswick in February 1945 and was disbanded there two weeks before the end of the war. Still at Garz on the island of Usedom on the Baltic coast (the site, incidentally, of the Peenemünde V2 rocket test-centre), the instructors of II./JG 110 flew operational sorties against the Red air force along the River Oder front during the opening weeks of 1945 before the Gruppe's disbandment in mid-February. At Wesendorf, north of Berlin, III./JG 110 survived until mid-March, when its members were remustered as ground troops to take part in the defence of the German capital.

10: 1./Ergänzungsjagdgruppe West *(1 Squadron/Replacement Fighter Group West)*

The equivalent of the RAF's operational training units (OTUs), the Luftwaffe's Ergänzungs units underwent a succession of changes as the war progressed. Initially, each Jagdgeschwader was ordered to set up its own Ergänzungsstaffel (replacement squadron). Usually equipped with 'war-weary' machines retired from service by its parent unit, and staffed by Geschwader pilots

– either on temporary attachment, resting from operations or recovering from wounds – the job of the Ergänzungsstaffel was to give newly qualified trainees from the fighter schools a 'final polish' to prepare them for front-line service.

JG 2's Ergänzungsstaffel was activated at Octeville, on the French channel coast near Le Havre, in mid-October 1940 under the command of Oberleutnant Horst Steinhardt. Towards the end of March 1941 this Ergänzungs unit was raised to Gruppe status. A Gruppenstab (Stab/ErgGr JG 2) was formed under Major Jürgen Roth. The original Ergänzungsstaffel now became 1./ErgGr JG 2 and a new 2./ErgGr JG 2 was added. The former adopted the role of an Einsatzstaffel (operational squadron), flying defensive patrols along the Channel coast, while the latter took over the duties of the Ausbildungsstaffel (training squadron), transferring to the quieter environs of Cazaux in southern France for the purpose.

In February 1942 all the Ergänzungs units were the subject of a major reorganization. Removed from the direct control of their parent Geschwadern, the Staffeln were now amalgamated into three autonomous Ergänzungsjagdgruppen: Ost, Süd and West (east, south and west) of three-four Staffeln each. However, the individual Staffeln retained their connections to, and continued to supply pilots for, their own particular Geschwader. The reorganization of February 1942 resulted in 2./ErgGr JG 2, now under the command of Hauptmann Hermann Hollweg, becoming 1./Ergänzungsgruppe West. At the same time the Staffel was transferred from Cazaux to Mont de Marsan, south of Bordeaux and close to the French Biscay coast.

At the end of 1942 the somewhat cumbersome 'Ergänzungs' prefix was dropped from the unit title, which now became 1./Jagdgruppe West. In April 1943 the unit, under its new Staffelkapitän, Oberleutnant Wilhelm Hobirk, moved south to Tarbes at the foot of the French Pyrenees. It was here, in May

1944, that it exchanged identities with 4./Jagdgruppe Süd.

Under its new designation the Staffel departed France the following month, June 1944, transferring first to Hohensalza and then to Neuruppin, some thirty-five miles to the northwest of Berlin. Yet more restructuring in November 1944 saw the four 'compass-point' Jagdgruppen (a Jagdgruppe Nord [North] having been created in September) combined to form Ergänzungs-jagdgeschwader 1. Jagdgruppe Süd was redesignated II./EJG 1, with 4./JGr Süd now becoming 8./EJG 1.

Late in January 1945 II./EJG 1, based at Schönwalde on the northern outskirts of Berlin, flew escort for the Luftwaffe Stukas and ground-assault aircraft attacking the Red Army as it advanced on the German capital. In mid-February 8./EJG 1, still commanded by the now Hauptmann Hobirk, withdrew to Ottingen, east of Bremen, where it was finally disbanded.

11: I./Jagdgeschwader 2 'Richthofen' (*1st Group/Fighter Wing 2 Richthofen*)

I./JG 2 was rightly proud of its premier place as the oldest fighter unit in the Luftwaffe. It could trace its history right back to 1930 – even before the birth of the Luftwaffe proper – when the German army secretly established three flying units. These were disguised to the outside world as Reklamestaffeln (advertising squadrons) and were ostensibly employed for aerial advertising purposes.

When the Luftwaffe officially came into being on 1 April 1934 it was one of these three Reklamestaffeln that was selected to form the nucleus of the new air arm's first fighter Gruppe. Initially known simply as the Fliegergruppe Döberitz (Air Group Döberitz) after its base to the west of Berlin, the unit was awarded the honour title, Richthofen on 14 March 1935.

Just over a year later, on 1 June 1936, the Luftwaffe introduced a three-figure system of unit designation, which resulted in the Fliegergruppe Döberitz becoming the first Gruppe of Jagdgeschwader 132 Richthofen (I./JG 132). Between then and the outbreak of war in 1939, a time of rapid expansion and a confusing multiplicity of redesignations within the Luftwaffe, the Jagdgeschwader 'Richthofen' was used to provide cadres for numerous other new fighter, Zerstörer and dive-bomber units. Having reached a peak strength of four Gruppen in 1938, the Geschwader had been reduced back down to its one original Gruppe by the outbreak of hostilities on 1 September 1939.

Operating now as I./JG 2, the Gruppe did not participate directly in the Polish campaign, but was instead retained at Döberitz to augment the aerial defence of Berlin in the event of allied bombing raids. It did, however, play a prominent role in both the Battles of France and Britain as part of General der Flieger (later Generalfeldmarschall) Hugo Sperrle's Air Fleet 3.

Following the Battle of Britain, I./JG 2 spent very nearly the whole of the next three-and-a-half years in northwest France, where it constituted the first line of defence against allied air incursions into occupied Europe. These grew steadily in strength and diversity, requiring the Gruppe to operate both at low level against roving enemy fighter-bombers and at high altitude against the four-engined Fortresses and Liberators of the American 8th AF.

From February to April 1944 the Gruppe was deployed, via the south of France, to Italy. Here it saw action against the allied forces attacking Cassino and attempting to break out of the Anzio beachhead. Returning to France immediately prior to the invasion of Normandy, I./JG 2 was almost wiped out in the weeks following D-Day. At least thirty-five pilots were killed or missing, plus many more wounded, before they were finally withdrawn to Germany at the end of August 1944.

Back on home soil for the first time in more than four years, I./JG 2 took up residence at Merzhausen to the northwest of

Frankfurt. The Gruppe was heavily involved in the defensive fighting on the western front during the autumn and winter of 1944. It took part in both the Ardennes counter-offensive (the 'Battle of the Bulge') and Operation Bodenplatte, the Luftwaffe's disastrous New Year's Day attack on allied airfields in France and the Low Countries on 1 January 1945. With fifteen pilots killed, missing or captured, I./JG 2 suffered the highest casualty rate of any of the Gruppen involved in the latter action.

Despite Merzhausen being extensively damaged by allied bombing, I./JG 2 remained there until the end of March 1945. Continuing to fly missions against increasingly heavy odds, it was during this period that the Gruppe lost its only Kommandeur to enemy action in nearly six years of war when Hauptmann Franz Hrdlicka was shot down by US fighters northeast of Frankfurt on 23 March. The following month I./JG 2 retired briefly into Czechoslovakia before returning to Germany, where it surrendered to American troops at Straubing near Regensburg.

INDEX

INDEX

INDEX